In Search
of
C.S. Lewis

Contributors

Patricia (Thomson) Berry
Norman Bradshaw
H.C. Chang
Rosamund Cowan
E.L. Edmonds
Jill Freud
W.R. Fryer
Patricia Heidelberger
David Hunt
Muriel Jones
Kathryn Lindskoog
Malcolm Muggeridge
Peter Philip
Joan Pile
Ruth Pitter
Alan Rook
Erik Routley
George Sayer
Stephen Schofield
A.J.P. Taylor
Kenneth Tynan
Naoyuki Yagyu

In Search of C.S. Lewis

Edited by Stephen Schofield

author of *Musketoon*

Interviews with
Kenneth Tynan, A.J.P. Taylor, Malcolm Muggeridge and others who knew Lewis

Contains previously unpublished letters and photographs . . .

BRIDGE PUBLISHING, INC.
Publishers of:
LOGOS • HAVEN • OPEN SCROLL

Cover illustration by Juliet Pannett.

In Search of C.S. Lewis
Copyright © 1983 by Bridge Publishing, Inc.
Printed in the United States of America
Library of Congress Catalog Card Number: 83-72224
International Standard Book Number: 0-88270-544-X
Bridge Publishing, Inc., South Plainfield, NJ 07080

To Esther, Elaine, Ted and Wood, with love.

For permission to use various C.S. Lewis and W.H. Lewis letters, quotations and drawings, the editor and publisher are profoundly grateful to:

Collins, Sons & Co. Ltd., London;

Harcourt, Brace, Jovanovich Inc., New York;

Macmillan Publishing Co., New York;

Harper & Row, Publishers, San Francisco;

The Reverend Walter Hooper, trustee of the C.S. Lewis estate;

Royds Barfield, Solicitors, London;

William Heinemann Ltd., London;

Wm. B. Eerdmans Publishing, Grand Rapids, Michigan;

Zondervan Publishing House, Grand Rapids, Michigan;

Hodder and Stoughton, London;

Curwen, Carten and Evans, Solicitors, London;

The Reporter Magazine Company, New York;

The Illustrated London News;

CSL The Bulletin of the New York C.S. Lewis Society;

The Reverend Dr. Erik Routley;

Desclée de Brouwer, Paris;

Johannes Verlag, Einsiedein, West Germany;

Charles Scribners Sons, New York;

The American Scholar, Washington, D.C.;

Iwanami Shoten, Publishers, Yokohama;

Verlag Herder, Freiburg, West Germany.

Contents

Preface

Who Was Lewis?

Clive Staples Lewis was an Oxford don who wrote books for children, for scholars, and for general readers. Since his death in 1963 the total world sales of his books have accelerated, now approaching a staggering fifty million copies.

As a Canadian journalist touring England on a bicycle in May, 1950, I lunched with him once, alone at Magdalen College. He was easy. He made me forget who he was. And he was then considered the greatest man in Oxford.

At the precocious age of twelve he wrote a complete novel. At sixteen he became an atheist. At thirty-two, at the end of a long and difficult process, and with great reluctance, he reverted to Christianity, and spoke and wrote about his discoveries.

This was sensational—both on the air and in print.

First on the BBC. Lewis said that it was probably because he was a layman and because he had been an atheist that the BBC offered him the opportunity to broadcast four ten-minute talks. This was for August, a minimum-listening month, and it was during wartime. It was not a great gamble for the BBC. The surprising thing is that a highly intellectual don—talking about the universe!—broke through to more than a million and prompted a flood of mail. More talks followed. His fame grew.

Another breakthrough occurred in a different way. Emerging one morning from church, of all places, an idea for a book came to his mind. The idea was simply to let the devil do the talking. And so Lewis wrote it, showing the easiest way to anger, misery, divorce and suicide, in thirty-one lessons. These are written in the form of letters from one devil to another, and they show how gleefully the devil laughs at each conquest. This little book, *The Screwtape Letters,* sold more than half a million copies, and for the first time in his life Lewis saw money rolling in. To celebrate, he gave money away in a haphazard fashion to various charities and individuals. He did this so much that to prevent chaos, his lawyer arranged for two-thirds of his income to be paid automatically to a charitable trust. This conformed to Lewis's view that for a Christian, the only safe rule is to give away more than one can afford. Thus went the profits from the books that flowed from the wondrous fecundity of his imagination and the breadth of his learning, and his facile pen. He continued with scholarly books and a children's series. Both flourished.

At his home in Headington he lived with his brother, Major Warren Lewis. Each summer the brothers went on a walking tour. "And jolly good fun they were too," Major Lewis told me. At home they had no television. Lewis never listened to the radio. On Sundays the brothers usually played a complete symphony on records; otherwise, they would read in the evenings and have a cup of tea before going to bed.

Rather suddenly, at the age of fifty-eight, Lewis surprised everyone by getting married. It was an uncommonly happy marriage, as it transpired, and lasted for about three years.

About the same time Lewis contracted osteoporosis, a bone disease. It steadily worsened. Other ailments aggravated his condition, and about three years after his wife died he knew that he too was facing death. "I have done all I wanted to do," he remarked to his brother one evening, "and I'm ready to go." In spite of all his woes, and he had plenty, he wrote more than forty books, mostly in spare time, in all a magnificent achievement.

Why was he not made a professor at Oxford?

Why was it considered wrong for him to have so many readers?

Why was he prejudiced against women?

And against Americans?

And why did he marry a dying American with two sons?

This book is an attempt to shed new light on Lewis, chiefly through friends and pupils. Some have written reminiscences. Others, I have interviewed, and a few chapters I have written myself, as indicated.

It is not all favorable. Some Lewis enthusiasts will not like this book, at least certain parts of it. I cannot help that. As far as I can ascertain, it is all true. And surely that is what Lewis would have wanted. As one pupil says, "It would be his wish: 'Speak of me as I am; nothing extenuate, nor aught set down in malice.'"

—Stephen Schofield
Dunsfold, Godalming
Surrey
England

Acknowledgments

The manuscript has been labored upon, shortened, lengthened and rewritten, again and again, over a period of about nine years. All contributors and letter writers have been most helpful. And to these must be added a number of others:

Owen Barfield, Lewis's friend;
James Como of the City University of New York;
Harold Gresswell, a Yorkshire editor;
Clyde Kilby, founder of the Wade Collection at Wheaton College, IL;
Hugh MacLennan of McGill University;
R.G.L. Perkins, an English schoolmaster;
Reverend John Pridmore, chaplain of King Edward's School, Surrey;
Robert Siegel of the University of Wisconsin;
Chad Walsh of Beloit College, Wisconsin;
and Charles Wrong of the University of South Florida.

MAGDALEN TOWER

— 1 —

Part A: Lunch With Lewis

Stephen Schofield

In Oxford one morning I parked my bicycle against Magdalen Tower and entered the College to meet a don who had kindly invited me to lunch. He was already waiting—a rather bald man in creaseless flannels and a battered jacket. "Mr. Scho*field?*" he queried, his inflection rising with a full-flavored Churchillian zing. I nodded; and without another word he led me to the dining room where we sat at a corner table for two. During the meal and afterwards, for about an hour, he gave me his entire attention such as I had never received from anyone. When he spoke his eyes shone; they gleamed, they were lustrous. His presence stimulated me. Such was my first impression of Lewis.

I had just written to say that I was a Canadian journalist and would be grateful if I could see him sometime; he replied by inviting me to lunch.

He drank a pint of ale with lunch, and afterwards we settled in leather armchairs. I asked if I could light my pipe. "Do!" he boomed out the word. This was in 1951 when he was at the height of his fame, though I did not know that. I only knew him as the author of a clever little book and I thought he might merit a newspaper column.

Who's Who listed his hobby as walking. I asked about that. He smiled and said he enjoyed walking with his brother in Ireland—"In *Northern* Ireland," he added quickly.

Did he ever do any climbing with ropes? "Oh, no," he said.

Did he care for any American writers? Yes, he liked Robert Frost and Emerson; but he said he "read very little contemporary writing."

1

Had he not tried Thomas Wolfe? "No," he said, "I don't know him." An odd contrast between Wolfe and Lewis is that they were both writers who could no more stop writing than prevent their hair from growing; but Wolfe loathed writing. Lewis enjoyed it.

I had just been to the House of Commons to hear Winston Churchill speak. As I sat there the news was announced that President Truman had dismissed General MacArthur as Commander of UN forces in Korea. Churchill rose and extolled MacArthur's "brilliant services throughout the Great War, and since." That lovely, rich voice came to me so clearly, though I am deaf and I was sitting at the back of the press gallery. This was due to the amplification through loud-speakers concealed in the upholstery of the seats in the galleries. I told Lewis all about this and he, leaning towards me, listened as though the publication of his next book depended on hearing every word.

We simply chatted. Before interviewing illustrious people I usually typed out a list of questions in duplicate. For Lewis I did not. This was due to my own ignorance of the intellectual giant who all but held out a chair for me to sit down on. He! For me! I did not linger long. My last impression is of his warm smile as we shook hands before leaving.

Part B: Exhilaration

Kenneth Tynan

Mr. Tynan, a well-known English dramatist and critic, died in California in 1980 at the age of fifty-three. Gore Vidal, an American book reviewer and author, paid an affectionate tribute to him in a long article in The London Observer, *which had employed Mr. Tynan as a critic. For some years—1964 to 1974—he was Lord Laurence Olivier's right-hand man at the National Theatre. Tynan wrote books about the National Theatre. When I interviewed him in his house in London in the late nineteen-seventies, I thought he looked weak and pale. We sat on a couch in the salon.*

"Well, Mr. Tynan," I said, "you may remember George Bailey,[1] the American from Columbia University, when he was at Oxford?"

"Oh, yes, indeed. He was with me at Magdalen."

"He wrote this piece in *The Reporter,*[2] mostly reprinted in a book.[3] Did you read it, Mr. Tynan?"

"No."

"Bailey said, 'If Lewis had any favorites among us, they were Kenneth Tynan and Tim Hardy. This, perhaps, because both Tynan and Hardy were very good at reading verse with an actor's sense of rhythm.'[4] Is that right, Mr. Tynan?"

"No. Completely untrue. That isn't true because I had—and still do have—a very bad impediment in my speech."

"Like that of King George VI?"

"As bad as that, yes. I had a very heavy stammer, so heavy that I could not read my essays for Lewis out loud at all. I was very, very shy of Lewis at first. It would have taken me the whole hour of a tutorial to read my essay aloud because I would be hesitating so much. So he very kindly read them aloud to me. And in fact it became quite a test to write essays that could survive being read in that wonderfully resonant voice of his. I found I was writing better because I knew he was going to be reading

3

them to me. It was a great treat for me to hear my own words read aloud by Lewis. So George [Bailey] is completely wrong when he says—"

"Bailey must have done that out of sympathy for you."

"Absolutely."

"You overcame the stammer later?"

"I was able to overcome it when I was making speeches or when I was acting. But it still comes over me when I am with someone I am in awe of."

"Not Olivier?"

"When I first knew Olivier, yes; but not since I have gotten to know him."

"Well, now, Mr. Tynan, Bailey has this to say about you, 'Tynan did not like Lewis as a tutor . . . .' "[5]

"Oh, that is absolute nonsense. It is quite false to say I did not like Lewis as a tutor. Lewis was undoubtedly the most powerful and formative influence of my whole life up to that point. Without any doubt at all."

"Then how did Bailey get the impression that you didn't like him?"

"I can't imagine. It is absolutely false. I found Lewis the most impressive mind I had ever seen in action. He had the breadth and clarity of mind of Dr. Johnson. He had the persuasiveness of Samuel Johnson without the bullying; but he had the same swiftness to grasp the heart of a problem and the same sort of pouncing intelligence to follow it through to its conclusion. I found him immensely invigorating, stimulating and inspiring. And I would say that his book on Sixteenth Century Literature[6] in the Oxford History is the most brilliant book of any literary criticism to have been published in my adult lifetime. It is a marvelous book and I heard most of the opinions expressed when he was my tutor."

"What about this other story of Bailey's—Lewis on the BBC talking about the act of love?[7] Is it right?"

"It simply isn't accurate. The true story is that I was preparing a program called 'Eros in the Arts,' which was about erotic literature; and I had often talked to Lewis about this. The man who was doing the interviewing was a famous writer who believed that sexual liberty in word and thought was desirable for literature, and he said, 'Who can I interview? Who is an intelligent man who would take the opposite point of view?'

"I said, 'C.S. Lewis would.'

"And he replied, 'Oh, but surely he is just a boring old Christian thinker?'

"I said, 'No, he is a man of the most brilliant and vivacious mind.'

"This chap then remarked, 'But I'm sure he will just trot out the old Christian, Puritan ideas.'

"I said, 'No, he won't. I don't know what arguments he will give, but it will surprise you.'

"And so the interviewer and I went to see Lewis in Headington. We came with our film unit into his house and the interviewer said, 'Tell me, Professor Lewis, what do you think of the use of four-letter words in literature?'

"Lewis answered, 'I find them objectionable because they are not erotic enough.' Not that they were too erotic, but that they weren't erotic enough.

"This completely bewildered the interviewer, who asked 'What do you mean?'

"Lewis responded, 'Well, if you look at the ancient poets you will find that when they are describing the act of love they never use four-letter words, because four-letter words do not arouse the senses. They always use images, and metaphors and similes. You will find that in ancient literature four-letter words are confined to scurrility and abuse.'

"Now this was a brilliant argument and it completely baffled the interviewer who said, 'I think we had better stop the cameras. I will think again.'

"And then George is quite right. Lewis went on to say, 'If you wish to describe the act of love in detail, you are restricted to the language of the nursery, the language of the operating theater, or the language of the gutter, and you may not wish to bring in any of these.'

"Then the interviewer said, 'But surely it is possible to describe physical activities in words?'

"Lewis replied, 'Can you describe to me, sir, how a pair of scissors works?'

"And the interviewer said, 'Well, it is a piece of steel that has little . . . ,' and he realized he could not describe it.

"Lewis said, 'If you can't describe a pair of scissors, now can you describe the act of love?' That is the full story."

"Well," I said, "I'm grateful to you for putting it straight, Mr. Tynan. And now may I ask something about Lewis's work? What do you think of his idea that if we don't praise God we're missing the greatest experience?"[8]

"Well, I am not myself a doctrinal Christian. If I were to approach Christianity it would be because Lewis had pushed me in his books, though, of course, he never tried to do so in his private life. He never brought his religious beliefs into his literary tutorials. But I find his finest Christian book is the little one called *Miracles*,[9] which he really, in moments of doubt, brought me very close to thinking if there is a Christian God, he must be very like the God that Lewis writes about. And I have seen him arguing with scientists and rationalists, and defeating them more often than any other Christian I have heard."

"How did he appear to you during tutorials, did he have any particular characteristics?"

"I was at Magdalen from 1945 to 1948 and there were some very cold winters and Lewis would usually receive me in wintertime in a woolen cardigan with an old dressing gown on top of it. It was extremely cold. We had hardly any electricity or coal because it was post-war England and things were very bad. And occasionally in the middle of a tutorial he would quite unceremoniously get up and go to the next room and relieve himself in a chamber pot, and then come back and continue the tutorial.

"And he would always puff on his pipe as a means of punctuating his argument. At times he would use it almost as a weapon to gesture with. If I asked him a question which momentarily baffled him, it would mysteriously go out, and while he was relighting it he would also be preparing a definitive, watertight answer.

"He had the most astonishing memory of any man I have ever known. In conversation I might have said to him, 'I read a marvelous medieval poem this morning, and I particularly liked this line.' I would then quote the line. Lewis would usually be able to go on to quote the rest of the page. It was astonishing.

"Once when I was invited to his rooms after dinner for a glass of beer, he played a game. He directed, 'Give me a number from one to forty.'

"I said, 'Thirty.'

"He acknowledged, 'Right. Go to the thirtieth shelf in my library.' Then he said, 'Give me another number from one to twenty.'

"I answered, 'Fourteen.'

"He continued, 'Right. Get the fourteenth book off the shelf. Now let's have a number from one to 100.'

"I said, 'Forty-six.'

" 'Now turn to page forty-six! Pick a number from one to twenty-five for the line of the page.'

"I said, 'Six.'

" 'So,' he would say, 'read me that line.' He could always identify it—not only by identifying the book, but he was also usually able to quote the rest of the page. This is a gift. This is something you can't learn. It was remarkable.

"But the great thing about him as a teacher of literature was that he could take you into the medieval mind and the mind of a classical writer. He could make you understand that classicism and medievalism were really vivid and alive—that it was not the business of literature to be 'relevant' to us, but *our* business to be 'relevant' to *it*. It was not a matter of dead books covered in dust on our shelves. He could make you see the world through the eyes of a medieval poet as no other teacher could do. You felt that you had been inside Chaucer's mind after talking to him. As a teacher he was incomparable.

"He always expected me to get a first-class degree and I got a second-class degree. On the Anglo-Saxon paper I was very bad. This let me down. Lewis was very sympathetic and he wrote me a charming letter afterwards telling me not to worry about not having gotten a first-class degree. I should add that he was a very witty and funny man, deeply humorous, which is not often brought out by people who write about him."

"One other thing, Mr. Tynan. What would you say of Lewis's view, or perhaps I should say Milton's view, of the beautiful woman who wants to be admired? You must know his *Preface to Paradise Lost?*"[10]

"Yes, I think Lewis writing about *Paradise Lost* taught me more about Milton and it is the simplicity of his approach that made it so marvelous. He says Adam's sin was disobedience. It is as simple as that. Other critics have given long, metaphysical explanations of what

Adam's sin was. But it is Lewis who wrote that what Adam did was to disobey, that is the crime, and Eve's sin was murder, because she, by offering him the fruit, condemned him and herself to death."

"It was committing murder. Lewis makes that clear," I observed.

"In fact it was also suicide, was it not? Because she had already condemned herself to death by eating the fruit herself so she had virtually committed suicide. She had committed suicide and then murder by offering it to Adam. Now before you go can I just tell you a story of Lewis's humanity?"

"Of course. Please."

"In my last year at Oxford I went to Lewis and told him that I would have to postpone my final examinations which I was supposed to have in the summer of 1948. I said, 'Please, can I postpone them until the winter?'

"He asked, 'Why?'

"I told him that I had very bad lungs, a very bad bronchial condition (I still have), but at that time it was severe and I had been in and out of hospitals for several months, and I hadn't been able to work to the required standard. At the same time, about a month before the examinations, a girl with whom I was very much in love decided overnight that she would give me up. I had planned to marry her and we had even applied for a wedding certificate. But overnight she decided for her own good reasons that she preferred somebody else. The combination of my physical illness and this great emotional blow made me feel very bad. I came to Lewis and said, 'Not only do I want to postpone the examinations, I really don't see any reason for living—at least not now.' (One gets very dramatic about emotional episodes at that age.) I was in a real state of despair when I took my troubles to him.

"Lewis said, 'Tynan, am I right in thinking that you once told me that during the war, when you were about twelve years old, living in Birmingham, there was an air raid on the town?'

"I answered, 'Yes.' (We were heavily bombed in Birmingham.)

"Lewis reminded me of something else. 'Didn't you tell me that one plane dropped a land mine by parachute and that it nearly blew up your house, missing it only by inches?'

" 'Yes,' I admitted.

" 'Now if the wind had blown that bomb a few inches nearer your house, you would be dead. So ever since then—and that was seven years ago—all the time you have lived has been a bonus. It is a gift. It is a fantastic present you have been given. And now you are talking about giving up this incredible gift and you could have been dead for eight years. You have had eight years of life that you had no reason to expect. How can you be so ungrateful?'

"Suddenly I saw my little problems in perspective. He had remembered this story of the bomb which I had told him only casually years earlier. He had remembered it and he suddenly brought it up when I needed to realize how stupid my little despair was, especially when it was seen against the fact that I had survived for eight years when really I had every right to be dead. That helped me enormously. I saw my problems for the silly, little things they were. And I walked out of his room exhilarated and uplifted. A great man."

— 2 —

The Butcher

Alan Rook

Major Alan Rook is a Fellow of the Royal Society of Literature, and an internationally known wine taster and vineyard owner. He is also well known as a war poet. His Soldiers, This Solitude[1] *contains "Dunkirk," which was considered the finest poem inspired by the war. He has published six books of poetry. Two of these are:* We Who Are Fortunate *and* These Are My Comrades.[2] *Major Rook invited me to spend a weekend at his country manor, "Stragglethorpe Hall," on his vineyard estate in Lincolnshire. On a sunny afternoon, sitting on a veranda, overlooking the vineyard and garden, and with a colorful peacock strutting about, I told him something of my research and then asked for his own experience with Lewis.*

"Yes," he said, "I had Lewis as a tutor for about six months. After that he said to me, 'Rook, your mind and mine are too much alike. If you continue with me you'll become just another Lewis. You don't want that! You'd better go on to someone else.' Which I did. In all my dealings with Lewis I felt happy but incompetent. I'm sure we all did. Though kindly, he was not warm, and to be continually up against his ineluctable logic was distinctly chilling."

"You said in your letter that Lewis sometimes invited you for fruit and Madeira in his rooms—and you talked until the small hours of the morning!"

"Yes. On several occasions he invited me to dine with him at high table at Magdalen, and afterwards we would go across to his rooms for Madeira and dessert. The pattern was always the same. He would ask another chap, usually an undergraduate and usually a philosopher, to join us. And the three of us would pick out some philosophical concept and explore it in argument, often until five o'clock in the morning. We'd just go on until finally we fell silent. There was nothing more to say. It was always stimulating, although at the time I felt mentally depleted."

"This must have been just a few years before he wrote those 'Broadcast Talks' which are now the first part of *Mere Christianity*[3]—is that about right?"

"Yes, it was."

"Well, then, you may have helped him traduce atheism by pure logic—as he does in those talks?"

"We reached many conclusions. But I can't for the life of me remember what they were!"

"You said he gave you Madeira wine?"

"Usually. But very little. Just enough to lubricate our throats. It was not a party, you understand. There was no small talk, nor laughter nor light moments, nothing of what I would call humanity such as I experience when I'm talking to you, for example . . . . I never felt any warmth in my encounters with Lewis. No real human contact. It was purely intellectual and logical reasoning and facts. I think that's how he lived. Always thinking about something—deeper and deeper. He used us as a foil."

"You must have been an exceptional student."

"Well, in the world I grew up in—starting with a governess, then preparatory school and public school and living in France for a couple of years—going to Oxford seemed perfectly natural. I knew what I wanted to do. I wanted to read English, particularly Medieval English. I worked very hard—about twelve hours a day."

"Twelve hours a day!"

"Yes, studying in my rooms—very little time at lectures. Charles L. Wrenn, who marked our examination papers, told me later than in his twenty-five years of experience as an examiner, my English papers were the best he had ever marked."

"Did you ever go to the Inklings?"[4]

"Occasionally I was asked to join the Inklings, not, I think, by Lewis, but by Nevill Coghill or Ronald (J.R.R.) Tolkien. I never went. I would have felt out of place. They were all dons, older than myself, and I didn't then, and I don't now, really enjoy literary get-togethers. Perhaps I should have gone. I probably missed some very good talk."

"Did Lewis ever talk to you about himself?"

"Very seldom. Once he said, 'Rook, you think of me as a Medievalist and a scholar. You're making a mistake. I'm nothing of the sort. I'm a butcher—a rough and brutal man.' Those were his words. What he meant, I think, was that even in casual conversation at high table, chatting about one thing or another, he would suddenly demolish an argument like a butcher bringing down a meat cleaver—almost to the point of rudeness. I'm sure he didn't mean it. It was just his way. But it wasn't always popular! But I loved it in spite of the fact that I was often on the receiving end."

"Well, he was popular as a lecturer."

"Yes, he was."

"Why would you say he was popular, Mr. Rook? What was the attraction?"

"He cited facts. There were a lot of not-very-bright students who wanted someone to tell them the facts, as opposed to someone like Nevill Coghill, who would talk wittingly and charmingly about Chaucer or modern poetry, without really helping them much to answer examination questions. Many students wanted the facts distinctly presented, in the way Lewis did. A lot of women wrote down what they could as Lewis spoke, and they tried to memorize it. They knew this would be helpful in their finals. I wouldn't say Lewis was a good lecturer. He read word for word from his brief. For me, at least, he never really illuminated anything. I think I felt that, for him, poetry consisted of the poet's philosophy. I disagreed. You can't take an Elizabethan lyric and reduce it to a philosophical concept without leaving out the poetry. You've missed the point if you try."

"I don't suppose you were ever at the Kilns, Lewis's home in Headington?"

"Yes, he invited me there for tea sometimes."

"Really! He must have enjoyed your company. Of all the pupils I've met, you're the only one who was ever there. Did you meet Mrs. Moore

[Lewis's adopted mother] or her daughter?"

"No. No women at all. He invited me there for tea. I arrived just when Lewis and his brother returned from their walk and we sat down to a big tea—buttered toast and crumpets and cake—all set out on a round table. He did loosen up very slightly at tea, probably on account of his brother, a much simpler man. One might say that Lewis allowed the tone of conversation to drop about one notch below normal. He was a little more human, though never really warm, during these tea parties."

"Did you ever meet that Irish don, Enid Starkie, who led the campaign against Lewis for the professorship of poetry?"[5]

"Yes. I dined one evening at her college—Somerville. I sat next to her. I found her rather alarming. I felt perhaps she didn't like men."

"I don't suppose you ever met Lewis's wife?"

"No. I wasn't in Oxford then."

"What did you think of Lewis—of all people!—getting married?"

"I always assumed it must have been a marriage of compassion. I can't imagine Lewis marrying for any other reason. I can't imagine the erotic motive inducing him. I have learned since that she was dying of cancer, or thought to be dying of cancer, when they were married. That would seem to me to be perfectly in character with Lewis."

"I think you're right there on both counts. He did mention to one friend who was on the radio the other night, a woman, in fact—Stella Aldwinkle—that he 'couldn't imagine why anyone would want to marry a woman.'[6] Now what about your own poetry, Mr. Rook? When you had some poetry published, surely you sent Lewis a copy?"

"Yes, I did. He replied with a very serious letter of criticism; but encouraging too. He had many criticisms which I didn't agree with. But he concluded that I could feel well satisfied with my achievement. I was then still in Oxford."

"You never saw him again after you left Oxford?"

"Yes, once. At a meeting of the Royal Society of Literature at 11 Downing Street, when R.A.B.—now Lord Butler—was Chancellor of the Exchequer, and also President of the Society. Lewis was standing alone. He was short, you know, in stature. And he looked cross. I felt he didn't know what he was doing there, or why he had come. I went up to him and we talked. Then he said, 'Let's get out of here.' We left together.

And the last I saw of him was a small, tubby, bent figure with a heavy
walking stick, walking down Whitehall, looking for a tube."[7]

— 3 —

Impressions of a Pupil

Norman Bradshaw

> *As an undergraduate at Magdalen College in 1935,*
> *Mr. Bradshaw surprised Lewis by bringing a recorder to a*
> *tutorial, and playing it to suitable verses of poetry.*
> *Apparently no one else had ever done this. Years later,*
> *Lewis referred to it in a testimonial. In one of his finest*
> *books,* English Literature in the Sixteenth Century
> (excluding drama), *Lewis mentions Mr. Bradshaw as a*
> *"learned pupil." Most of Mr. Bradshaw's life has been spent*
> *in the academic world. He has been headmaster of two*
> *grammar schools. He recently retired from the headmaster-*
> *ship of the Royal Russell School, Addington, and is now*
> *with a publishing firm. He is an agreeable man, as Lewis*
> *remarks in the following letter of recommendation, and he*
> *has an aristocratic air. For this latter reason he is known to*
> *his intimates as "the Baron."*

Magdalen College, Oxford.
Dec. 4th, 1938

Mr. N. Bradshaw was my pupil while reading for the Final Honour
School of English Language and Literature. He is a man of untiring
industry and I think he came a little stale and tired to the examination, in
which, nevertheless, he was at the *top* of the Second Class. His
scholarship is accurate and sensitive and he is sufficient of a musician

17

and musical historian to illuminate his literary studies from that neglected angle. He is a *very* agreeable man to work with and I can recommend him unreservedly.

C.S. Lewis
Fellow and Tutor of Magdalen

When I arrived at his rooms in New Buildings he was usually reading and always smoking, generally a pipe. "Good morning, good morning," he would invariably say; and after listening to my essay, he would, in the Socratic method, ask me questions. Rarely would he say anything really encouraging and, though I began (and ended) by admiring his learning and logic ("this side idolatry," as Ben Jonson said of Shakespeare), the effect of his tutoring was, for a time, to make me uneasy, and tended to undermine my confidence in my own judgment and powers of reasoning.

He did not mean to be hurtful because he was fundamentally kind and courteous. But it seemed to me as though he was using his pupils as a whetstone on which to sharpen his own powers of dialectic argument, rather than, as I had hoped, helping us in a search for truth. It was almost like undergoing an operation. However, the pain of being driven into a corner by his logic was only temporary. After a long series of these "operations," one felt a good deal better. One's mind was immensely clearer in the end, although the recovery was slow.

I realized later that he had taught me to think, or at least to think much more clearly about *how* to think clearly, and my confidence returned. He taught me to be suspicious of the cliché, the glib phrase, the second-hand opinion; he led me to seek the precise definition, and to analyze subtly different shades of meaning.

He showed real interest in my own views when, at tutorial, I took some early sixteenth century poetry such as this:

> Whereto should I express
> My inward heaviness,
> No mirth can make me fain
> Till that we meet again.
> (Words ascribed to King Henry VIII.)

This did not sound like good poetry, but it had, I sensed, a kind of

18

rhythm waiting to be brought out which I felt to be suited to simple music such as I could play on my recorder. The verses, by themselves, were dead. The music brought them to life. To illustrate this I took my recorder to a tutorial and played suitable music for several verses. Evidently this was the first time an undergraduate had thus performed in his presence! He was agreeably surprised.

He suffered from a bladder weakness (caused by World War I service at the front). He used to get up, sometimes, in the middle of a tutorial and say, "Well, I must go and have a pee." This, in 1936, was felt by most pupils to be "ungentlemanly." Certainly it was very unusual and very surprising.

He appeared always, from policy, to keep his pupils at arm's length. But he would unbend after the final examinations, for one evening at least. He would have the scouts bring up dinner to his rooms for about twelve of us. After dinner we'd have a game, reading aloud a novel called *Irene Iddesleigh*[1] by Amanda M'Kittrick Ros. You can imagine what it was like: a very sentimental book in flowery language. The game was to see who could read the furthest without laughing. It made for a hilarious evening. Here is an extract:

> Speak! Irene! Wife! Woman! Do not sit in silence and allow the blood that now boils in my veins to ooze through cavities of unrestrained passion and trickle down to drench me with its crimson hue!

He told me he never read "undergraduates' poetry" and in 1938— though he changed his mind later—he was contemptuous of T.S. Eliot, saying that "The Waste Land" was little more than a "ragbag of quotations of the best lines of earlier poets." I had praised the line, "I had not thought death had undone so many." But he deflated me somewhat by referring to the Dante original, though I tried to defend the felicity of . . . [Eliot's usage]. He used to say that modern literature—that is anything later than Wordsworth—was not a suitable university subject. Contemporary writing, he would assert, is something not assessed by time; what is good in it, you—that is, his pupils—should be telling him. But, if I tried, he would seldom listen; he was not really interested.

I remember Lewis once attended a dinner to meet Walter de la Mare and A.L. Rowse. Lewis mentioned that he thought A.L. Rowse seemed to imagine that there was only one correct view on anything, and that was A.L. Rowse's.[2]

I often sensed a mysteriousness and ambiguity in Lewis' comments to me about sexual relationships, when such comments arose in tutorials, as they naturally would, in connection with literature. It seemed that, in him, there was a deep *sense* of guilt about regarding such relationships as having, even potentially, any great part to play in human happiness. He appeared actually to relish speaking of sexual love as merely the gratification of another appetite, on a par with eating and drinking, perhaps less pleasurable than these, and certainly on no higher plane in any sense. This attitude was, of course, usual among medieval theologians, as distinct from poets; and Lewis clarified it in the references to Thomas Aquinas, in his book, *The Allegory of Love*.[3] This work established him as the leading world authority on "Courtly Love," as indeed the first chapter is called. Courtly love is the sentiment, apparently first expressed in the Middle Ages, in which the lady is regarded more as a deity to be worshiped than either as a human being or an object to be possessed. Though Lewis pointed out the ambiguities of the sentiment, there is no doubt as to its widespread influence on human thought and conduct. It is the origin of the "romantic" love that became the normal (though often hypocritically held) ideal until the mid-sixties of this century, somewhat disguised and perverted by Victorian possessiveness and sentimentality and by that Dickensian worship of domesticity, satirized in such works as Richard Aldington's novel, *Death of a Hero*. According to Lewis, courtly or romantic love was an entirely new development in the human consciousness, replacing the older Greco-Roman and heroic-age view of women. Once, to my utter astonishment, Lewis said to me that though he had written at length about courtly love, he had done so, not (as I imagined) to praise it, but to describe its rise, suggest that it was an idolatrous and ephemeral sentiment, and to predict its eventual replacement by very different attitudes toward sexual matters. His prophecies as to the decline of "romantic" love have been abundantly justified since the time of his death.

What for the most part he expressed preference for, when I knew him, was the heroic-age camaraderie of warriors feasting in their hall, with bards reciting the exploits of those present—and no women in sight! Yet, at the same time, he gave me the impression of his having a nostalgic feeling that there was, after all, something good about courtly love. He was clearly fascinated by the subject or he could not have written the definitive work on it.

In *The Pilgrim's Regress*[4] are hints of deep conflicts within himself, symbolized by the "brown girls," one "divinely fair," and one of his obsessions: the unnaturalness of slender girls, and surprising prophecies of "unisex."[5] He spoke later, though, of finding the love at nearly sixty that he had missed at twenty. In *A Grief Observed,* he wrote in terms that suggest he experienced a fusion of some of the oversubtle distinctions of *The Four Loves.*[6] Did he at last, happily though so briefly, reconcile some warring or unresolved elements in his nature? Was woman no longer dangerous, because she was neither a "brown girl" nor one "divinely fair," neither a temptress nor a goddess, but a human being he came to love, and who "happened" to be a woman?

He would not, in my time, ever act as tutor to women. He seemed almost afraid of them. It was a standing joke at Magdalen that whenever he saw a woman enter the College he would run as fast as he could and lock himself in his rooms.[7] Once, when a friend became engaged, he referred to the engagement as "that fatal tomb of all lively and interesting men."[8] Much later, at Cambridge, it appears that Lewis would never accept invitations to address an audience of women.[9]

He would, of course, walk, walk, walk, and think, think, think, all the time. It could well be that much of what I regard as his finest work, *The Problem of Pain,*[10] or the early chapters of *Miracles,*[11] transpired from those daily, hard-thinking walks.

I remember during a walk of mine, in the early spring of 1936, entering the porch of an old church somewhere near Headington with two friends and finding C.S. Lewis sitting on a stone bench just inside the porch, and his brother sitting opposite him. They both had stout walking sticks. They were silent, meditating, motionless—almost like parts of the stone building, gazing straight ahead. We fled, tiptoe, in awe.

He liked to win. He liked to demolish an opponent's argument. When he was with friends, the Inklings, for instance, I imagine he was hearty and warm, hail fellow well met. But quite often, during or after dinner with other people, a point might crop up in conversation. Lewis would take up the argument and knock the other chap as flat as a house of cards. There was nothing left for him to say. He was down and out and speechless. And Lewis would sit back and take another sip of port. But that man might well have been, later, the very one whose good word could have tipped the balance for a professorship for Lewis.

In 1936 he said to me (quoting, perhaps) in a tutorial: "The so-called Renaissance produced three disasters: the invention of gunpowder, the invention of printing, and the discovery of America." In *Letters of C.S.Lewis* appear patronizing and disparaging references to Americans. After his war-time and post-war experience of food-parcels and the invasion of Magdalen College from the States, this last prejudice disappeared, as his *Letters* clearly show.

Also, I think Lewis was rather short-sighted to dismiss *all* the theories of psychologists from Freud onwards and, more harshly, the work of psychotherapists in healing. In particular it was unwise to ignore Jung, who in his later years devoted so much of his attention to literary art and whose conclusions were remarkably compatible in many ways with Lewis's views on myth, and with Christian teaching, though they were not, I suppose, so definitely anti-demythologizingly Christian for Lewis, in his most intransigent years, to admit that they had any new insights to offer. And it was, it was left to the philologist, Charles Wrenn, to introduce me to Maud Bodkin's *Archetypal Patterns in Poetry* (which opened more horizons than Lewis ever did) and for myself to find the books of Wilson Knight, which took me into quite new universes of literary appreciation. Yet it should have been the great "myth-man," Lewis himself, who could and should have done this. What another contradiction in the man! Whether the First World War did arrest certain aspects of his development, or whether there was a kind of proud independence about it all, I'm not sure. What I mean is illustrated in *Letters of C.S. Lewis* (March 26, 1940, p. 179), where he wrote, "Psychoanalysis. In talking to me you must beware, because I am conscious of a partly pathological hostility to what is fashionable." His own words reveal so much: ". . . partly *pathological*," This was true of his dress. The photograph of his tweed jacket and baggy, creaseless trousers in 1958 (Kilby: *Images*, p. 64) show little if any change from his attire in 1938 (*Letters of C.S. Lewis*, p. 214), which is substantially the

"Oxford bags" wear of the 1920s. Yet in the same book (p. 10) is a picture of Lewis in the elegant dashing clothes of 1919—another contradiction! A further example of this reaction to innovation occurs to me. About 1937 the vogue came in for having, at the top of your trousers, an overlap containing a hook that was supposed to fasten on to a large tailor's eye on the left-hand waist-band. Lewis's kept getting itself unhooked and one day he complained to me bitterly about this, expostulating, "It's like having a great flannel penis hanging out!"

I remember hearing that when a new chaplain had been appointed to a certain college, a friend said, "Isn't he rather Low Church, after his predecessor?"

"No!" replied Lewis. "Not low—*flat!*"

And yet he was not, in my view, unpopular because he was blunt. I never knew him to be rude or discourteous. Though he was devastating, I came to realize there was nothing personal about it. In public debate he would "floor" an opponent courteously, not apparently making the opponent appear foolish, but everyone could see that Lewis's mind was so obviously the more penetrating that he had in fact done so, not through rude malice, but through dislike of cant, and love of accuracy and truth. As a side effect, one was made to appear of inferior intelligence, and this was, I suspect, secretly disliked by some other academics.

Edmund Blunden, the poet, then a Fellow at Merton, once said to me at a dinner that Lewis's logic overpowered him. This was said with no animosity, for Blunden was a mild man, with neither ambition nor malice, and he did not go in for public argument. But it is symptomatic of what I as a pupil felt and probably of what some dons felt—and resented.

Another reason for his unpopularity was that he believed in the supernatural, in things unseen. After the war, Oxford philosophy became dominated by the "linguistic phenomenalists," inheritors of the logical positives. They held that a mental concept referred only to observable social behavior. Lewis was utterly unsympathetic to it. He was also uncompromising towards what was called "Christianity and water." He would not have it. He would have Christianity "mere," that is, basic, absolute, pure, and nothing else. I should add that he prepared me excellently to see that Christianity was not only a reasonable system of belief but probably the *only* reasonable one.

Lewis taught me to avoid being caught out by the behaviorist fallacy, which runs as follows: "There is no such thing as 'absolute truth.' It is no use believing in what person A says, because what he thinks is true is only the result of his upbringing and environment, which have conditioned him so that he cannot think otherwise. What he believes is simply part of his behavior pattern reflex."

To this Lewis was always ready with the classic refutation: "All right. But if this is so, then *your* belief in what person A thinks, is not 'true,' but is simply the result of *your* conditioning, *your* upbringing and environment, so that *you* can think in no other way. Why should I trust or believe in *your* conditioned thinking? Why on earth then should I imagine there is any point in listening to any of your remarks at all? There is no truth in them. They are simply *your* conditioned reflexes. Why should I expect truth from anyone else, either, since all I listen to are the opinions necessarily produced by *their* upbringing and environment?"[12]

I know of several dons with theological degrees who denigrated Lewis because he was not a professional theologian—that is, he had no degree in theology—and yet he was becoming a household name. This must have been very galling to the theologians who were seeking fame, and these despised him as a "non-professional popularizer." The really great scholars, of course—for instance, Professor Sir Godfrey Driver— were his friends.

Lewis told me in 1938 that he did not really like the thought of broadcasting, and when he appeared on "Any Questions?" he said very little; the discussion was too trivial. He preferred a live audience and like many shy people, he was a bit of an actor. His lectures were packed. I remember how the largest lecture room in the Schools dissolved in laughter when he referred to the two coy nymphs in Spenser's *Faerie Queene,* ducking in the water: "They were obviously," he said, "called Cissie and Flossie!"

Although everyone realized that he knew more about English and poetry than anyone else, he was passed over for professorships. There were reasons for his unpopularity. One was that he had no time for small talk. Another was that by broadcasting and writing he had allowed his name to become a household word. And there had long been a general feeling in England of what might be called automatic progress: that morally and materially we were becoming and were bound to become better and better. Most people agreed. But not Lewis. He was skeptical about it, and about the amount of fundamental improvement that could be brought about by "social engineering." When I once read him a poem by Stephen Spender about the unemployed of the Great Depression, a poem I found, and still find, very moving: "In railway halls . . . ," he was absolutely untouched and said he found nothing in it. Parochial social problems, such as mass unemployment, seemed never to enter his consciousness. This was also to earn him, after the Second World War, the label of "escapist." He came to be regarded as a Tory (Conservative) reactionary whose standpoint was a stumbling block to the left-wing agnostics who gradually supplanted the unusual intellectual mixture of open-mindedness and liberal High Anglicanism that I found there, in, for example Canon Adam Fox, Professor Sir Godfrey Driver, P.V.M. Benecke, President George Gordon, H.M.D. Parker, Sir John Wolfenden and (earlier) Professor J.A. Smith, of whom Lewis wrote in his preface to *The Allegory of Love*[13]: "To have lived in the same college staircase with him was itself a liberal education."

Adam Fox related to me that at one time, soon after Lewis's "conversion," he and Lewis together with J.A. Smith were often the only three partaking of breakfast in the Senior Common Room after attending the early morning celebration of Holy Communion in Magdalen Chapel.

Lewis was interested in his pupils, not as persons, but, by deliberate policy, as well as inclination, only so long as they baited him and allowed him to win an argument. He taught me little that directly increased my appreciation of literature; indeed, to some extent he turned me away, for a time, from any great interest in the subject, in favor of philology and philosophy. He was not discourteous, but sometimes you sensed a certain impatience and almost arrogance. When grovelling before him because I'd forgotten to attend a tutorial, he waved away my apologies, "I'm not your schoolmaster!" The tone said unequivocally, "It's *your* loss, not mine; but don't waste my time!" He used to catch a bad bout of influenza once a year, generally in February, and, after you'd climbed the wooden, uncarpeted steps to his rooms, you'd find pinned to his door a note saying, "Mr. Lewis is indisposed and regrets that he cannot hold any tutorials this week." We were not surprised. At the previous week's "tute" the unusual irritability had indicated that the annual visitation of the flu virus was imminent. I remember having, in 1936, an Old English tutorial with him, together with Peter Philip. In those days we had individual one-to-one tutorials in literature, but in our first terms, language tuition was given in pairs. At one stage, when we'd both been particularly obtuse about Verner's or Grimm's Law, he rounded on us and exploded, "Really! Your work seems to show an absolute ignorance of the most elementary facts about sound changes!" (He'd forgotten what he himself had written in November, 1922: ". . . why physiology should form part of the English School I really don't know . . . ."[14]) I'm sure he was right about our work, alas! It was rare, but to be savaged by a Lewis sickening for flu was a cataclysmic experience!

Perhaps I should have gained more from him if I'd been older. I'm sure he was a better tutor to men returning from the Forces after the war. But then I'd have missed the one hour a week tutorials alone with him, for three years (the numbers did not run to this again after 1945 for a long time), tutorials that stretched my brain, even if almost to breaking point and despair. Did he demoralize (1) me as well as stretch (2) me? Yes. Which was more important? Did I get over (1) but retain the value of (2)? John Wain has summed it up so well: "Lewis had no innate sympathy with the kind of mind that shrinks away from dispute and develops its ideas best in an atmosphere of encouragement."[15] Yes, if I had not been his pupil, would I have ever come across that greatly neglected and masterly book, *The Pilgrim's Regress,* with its unforgettable summary of his best teaching, "What does not satisfy when we find it, was not the thing we were desiring,"[16] and with so much of his best verse: "The filling of the moment's want

And to be free from pain,"[17]

and a line that Ronald Fryer and I can never forget, "The tether and the pang of the particular."[18]

So there is Lewis, that enigma, that paradox; that extraordinary being: courteous yet harsh; gentle, yet a "butcher"; arrogant, obsessive about his own pride, yet humble; sensuous yet puritanical; learned yet ordinary; magnanimous yet limited; sympathetic yet intolerant; wise yet blind; simple but complicated; above all, so contradictory, like human nature itself.

Postscript

Lewis was an earlier pupil of George Gordon, President of Magdalen in the late thirties and Professor of Poetry. Lewis mentions him in the *Letters*. He succeeded, as President, Sir Herbert Warren, who appointed Lewis in the manner described in *Surprised by Joy*.[19] Sir Herbert's snobbery was still a joke when I was up. There is an old Magdalen story that, when the Prince of Wales (later King Edward VIII and then the Duke of Windsor) was known to be at Magdalen, the Emperor of Japan wrote to Sir Herbert and entered his son, His Imperial Highness Prince Chichibu, who subsequently became a member of the college. However, the Emperor of Japan wrote to Sir Herbert, "Dear Mr. President, I hope you will take great care of the Prince because he is the Son of God."

The President replied: "Your Celestial Majesty, You may rest assured of our care for the Prince; this college has 500 years of experience in educating the sons of gentlemen"!

— 4 —

Disappointment at Cambridge?

W.R. Fryer

Mr. Fryer was one of Lewis's pupils at Oxford. The dons called Mr. Fryer stupor mundi (the astonishment of the world) because of the length of his essays, forty minutes of reading time, the longest ever known. After graduation Mr. Fryer served with the British Army and then joined the faculty of history at the University of Nottingham. He is now Professor Emeritus, Retired.

I studied history at Magdalen from 1935 to 1938. Lewis taught, not only the students of English, but also the historians, students of political science—Aristotle to Lenin, more or less all the way. Going to Lewis for political science, I found him—not surprisingly—the only good *tutor* (not the only good *scholar,* the others too were important scholars, and they were very, very well-meaning and friendly too; but Lewis was the only good *tutor*) among the men who taught me at Oxford.

He wasn't only good. He was superhuman in the range of his knowledge and in the height of his intellectual vision; and to me, both then and afterwards, he was not only friendly and encouraging, but super-hospitable, gentle, even tender. It was the experience of a lifetime to find that this great scholar and brilliant teacher, with his odd mixture of the English farmer's exterior and the mind of a polymathic prophet, was at once so bluff and yet so gentle, so razor-like in analysis and yet so tolerant, even so modest, in personal tone. He was so vastly well-informed about modern unbelief in all its phases, yet himself professing, quietly enough, the creed of "an orthodox Christian" (as he used to put it), and citing "a dominical saying"—words of our Lord—as settling any point to which they applied.

I know there was a rough side of Lewis too. Some of his writings suggest a dark, even terrifying imagination. I must regard this dark imagination as a weakness in his character, and no one who admired and venerated him, as I did, would wish to parade such a weakness. At the same time I don't wish to run away from the suggestion. I wish to paint him as I knew him, and that must be "warts and all." His dark imagination played only, as far as I know, upon the subject of evil, considered—as he did consider it—as in some way embodied in a person who was, to be sure, the devil, Lucifer, who fell to become the satanic majesty. (His *human* characters were hardly devils, even when he painted them as very bad indeed—Weston, the 'bent' scientist of Mars and Venus, and even the White Witch, the usurping Queen of *Narnia*— we are *sorry* for them in the end, for they are not only wicked but hapless. And Lewis, as the last of "Old Western Men," had not about him, that I know, even a faint whiff of the depraved sadistic interest which in the seventies boasts of its conquest of our sexual powers. His sexual attitudes seem to have been honest, down-to-earth and—this is the worst—*humdrum*).

He believed in the devil far too much for his own, or for his readers', good; I hardly say intellectually (that's a matter of philosophical opinion), but *imaginatively*. In *Mere Christianity*,[1] for instance, he says, mildly enough: "I know someone will ask me, 'Do you really mean, at this time of day, to reintroduce our old friend the devil—hoofs and horns and all?' Well, what the time of day has to do with it I don't know. And I'm not particular about the hoofs and horns. But in other respects my answer is 'Yes, I do.'. . . If anybody really wants to know [the devil] better, I'd say to that person, 'Don't worry. *If you really want to, you will. Whether you'll like it when you do is another question.*' "[2]

The shivers already begin.

In *The Problem of Pain* Lewis writes, "Even if it were possible that the experience (if it can be called experience) of the lost contained no pain and much pleasure, still, that black pleasure which would be such as to send any soul, not already damned, flying to its prayers in nightmare terror." What may this black pleasure be? I don't know. But an earlier

30

Christian writer says, "I am convinced there is nothing in death or life, in the realm of spirits or superhuman powers, in the world as it is or the world as it shall be, in the forces of the universe, in heights or depths— nothing in all creation that can separate us from the love of God in Christ our Lord."[3]

In *That Hideous Strength,* the diabolical powers physically invade our planet. They move a group of brilliant, but desperately mad scientists to plan the survival of a human being, simply *in his head.* The person concerned is a French murderer. He is executed upon the guillotine. They steal his head. They hang it up on a lamp bracket, complete with pipes, cylinders, and what not, to convey to it oxygen, saliva, vital juices, so that (when they wish it to do so) it can speak, think, will and issue orders. A young Oxford sociologist, who mistakenly wishes to join this group, is solemnly introduced to "Our Head." It speaks to him from its lamp bracket, ghastly pale and concealed behind dark glasses, like Louis XIV in all his glory. The young man goes outside asweat and trembling in every limb; he is violently sick. In fact, this is not a triumph of science at all. The Head has not really been kept alive. It is an illusion created by the diabolical powers. But there is nothing illusory about the evil which the head embodies. When the game is evidently up, the head speaks without being invited. It says, "I want a *sacrifice.*" The other members of the group lay hold of the brilliant Italian who had planned the rescue of "Our Head"; they hurry him under a little guillotine which stood at the top of the hatch between two rooms. They cut his head off there and then, and offer it as an oblation to "Our Head." The novel ends happily. The good Angels ("Eldila"), decent human beings, etc., are reconciled. I was over forty when I read this book. I burned my copy of it. Our little daughter was about three. I did not care to let a copy of it remain in the house where she was to grow up. The experience of reading this book in a real sense *broke* me.

I agree with Norman Bradshaw when he mentions Lewis's comment on A.L. Rowse, and adds that Lewis was equally sure that Lewis's judgment was infallible. One always knew where Lewis stood, and that Lewis *knew* he was right. Norman Bradshaw and I had one glorious, comical moment over this when we went to see Gilbert and Sullivan's "Gondoliers" just before the Final Schools started. We were amused when the Grand Inquisitor looked *exactly* like Lewis, with his high-colored face and unself-consciously masterful attitudes. But when he started to sing, in Lewis's deep and confident tones:

> Of that there is no possible doubt,
> No possible, probable shadow of doubt,
> No possible doubt whatever . . . ,

he had us both rolling in the aisles.

Not long after Lewis's inauguration at Cambridge he wrote to John Lawlor that his medieval mission there had been a "flop *d'éstime.*" I feel these words have a ring of truth. I have no ground to doubt that the Cambridge authorities were very nice to him; but no amount of good intention on their part is likely to have obviated two major difficulties: Lewis was a lifelong Oxonian and had held his Fellowship at Magdalen, which he loved very dearly, for twenty-nine years. I have good reason to believe he would never have contemplated leaving Oxford, and Magdalen, for anywhere else whatever, not even Cambridge, had it not been for two special—and highly unwelcome—considerations.

For some years, he had groaned under what he viewed as the ascendancy established over college affairs at Magdalen by two other senior Fellows with whom his own *Weltanschauung* had nothing in common. They were political left-wingers, and unbelievers. This in itself would not have mattered to Lewis. He was not intolerant. But he came to feel that they were imposing their *Weltanschauung* in all kinds of college decisions to ends which he viewed as highly regrettable.

I don't know that Lewis was, in any vulgar sense of the term, professionally ambitious. But I gathered that, as the years ran on, it irked him to feel that not only had his own university not proposed to create a Chair for him, nor to elect him to an established Chair, but even his own college had not asked him to become its president. I think he felt his own college and university thought too lightly, not only of his scholarship, but, more important, of all that he had come to stand for in life. I conjecture that he was right. I could see how he was regarded by most of the people who mattered, in places far enough away from Oxford. Nobody questioned his learning or his attractive power. But the typical left-wingers and unbelievers, who already ruled our intellectual world, were 'put off' by Lewis. They seemed to regard him with a mixture of incredulity and alarm, as someone returned from the Middle Ages, with a whole array of awkward questions and a skill in debate which they certainly could not match.

The offer from Cambridge was, therefore, too flattering to refuse. But it seems only too probable that the reality of a special Chair at Cambridge was disappointing. The Cambridge English School had *never* made so much as the Oxford School of those philological and early elements in which Lewis rather specialized. He probably found the main currents of academic policy at Cambridge flowing irresistibly further away from all that he had valued. The intellectual and moral tone of Cambridge probably suited him no better than that of Oxford in his later years there. He found that he had changed to no advantage, except that of gaining a rather empty title.

His biographers mention that at Cambridge he was offered the chairmanship of the Faculty Board of English, and declined.[4] The chairmanship no doubt represented, *in outward semblance,* a flattering offer. But it would not have given him any effective *power*. It would have given him *influence* with people who were such as might have followed his line. But he no doubt felt that most of them would *not* have followed this line (to borrow a figure from J.M. Thompson, *apropos* something different altogether, Lewis would have found himself celebrating High Mass for an audience of convinced Puritans). Thus he would have had a lot of administrative work, of a kind he disliked, for no real advantage. And he was too old to make new friends in any sense comparable with his friends at Oxford.

Some characteristic *traits* come to mind, especially the jovial maleness and the assured, good-humored confidence which Lewis normally presented to the world. It demands heavy emphasis all the more, to the many readers who never met and knew Oxford dons, least of all Oxford dons as they were in the now-remote nineteen-thirties. The 'soft, spectacled Oxford manner' of Newman's time flourished (or dropped) still, a hundred years afterwards; only the 'band box neatness,' of which Newman had approvingly spoken, had in the meantime disappeared. And one had to deal still, in 1935 as in 1835, with a characteristic donnish being of pale, quiet, often silent presence, too often betraying, by some unevenness of step or by some awkward carriage of the arms, the man unaccustomed to life in the 'real' world, the man who knew less, and cared less, about this 'real' world than most inhabitants of monasteries; who when he spoke at all, spoke with a half a lisp, and with a curious mixture of trifling and defensive timidity; who, if he drank, certainly wouldn't drink beer; and if he smoked, certainly wouldn't smoke anything less exotic than Balkan Sobranie Turkish or Egyptian. After too many people like this, it was both a shock and an excitement to find the already famous Mr. Lewis, who used to be a dogmatic atheist and was now a pious Churchman, whose face was brilliant with color, whose voice was deep and loud, whose greeting was positively enthusiastic, whose step was firm and noisy; who *enjoyed* beer, and who smoked a perpetual succession of pipes and 'gaspers' (Will's Gold Flake, or 'yellow perils,' to be exact); who was quite likely to offer a pupil one of the latter, saying in the endearing syle of the World War I veteran, 'have a gasper . . .'; who used to carry all this formidable apparatus of masculinity right into the College Chapel and right into the near proximity of God's altar; to be its own self there, just as much as anywhere else. ("Mr. Lewis enters the Chapel," said the admiring and awe-struck Dick Hewitt once to me, "and the marble floors echo loudly to his iron tread. He goes up to his place in the stalls, and sinks on his knees with a resounding crash which makes all the wooden structure tremble. He opens his glasses case and closes it with a loud snap which reverberates around. Divine Service can now begin.")

But after all this, it was to be sure an even greater shock and excitement to discover that this so undonnish don, who spoke his mind in matters of learning with the same positive confidence with which he greeted a pupil on the staircase, or on the way to 'the bogs,' who was the very reverse of precious, and who had never experienced (one felt) the sad sensations of defensive timidity, was not less learned, not less brilliant, than his neo-monastic colleagues, but palpably more learned and brilliant. "There goes the great dragon," said Norman Bradshaw in tones of awe and endearment: "there goes the great leviathan."

There is only one person, it seems to me, to whom we really *need* to talk in the ranging, literary vein, with the hope of the long, the truly satisfying reply; and He is God. But God is *not* (despite everything to the contrary) 'a man in the next street'. He is, by definition, not a man at all; nor a girl. We know in effect nothing about Him, except that our reason assures us that He *is*; to post a letter to Him, in writing, or in 'the sighing of the human heart,' is to act as one of our own dear children; we know nothing of His strange providence, nothing of His ultimate design; Job knew the truth of all this long before any of us was hatched.

I return again and again to what I learned, certainly twenty-five years ago, from E.M. Forster's *A Passage to India*. The English ascendancy over there invite Professor Godbole to illustrate his own religious beliefs. He sings a little song in his own language. They boldly invite him to translate it into English. The old man says, 'In this poem, the lover says to God, Come, my Beloved, everything is prepared and I will welcome you. *But He will not come . . . .*'

This is what I think I have learned from life, and I wish I could have done better, for myself and all those dear to me. You can see how much I owe to C.S. Lewis, but also how much I differ from him. The Christians (I'm one of them, in my fashion) have *asserted* far too much. Even he, perhaps especially he, asserted too much: *for good,* to be sure. May the Unknown Beloved have great mercy for us all and not least for him: so learned, so well-wishing, so generous and outpouring with 'fags' [cigarettes] and pipes, with beer and wine and flowing, utterly convincing, manly, man-to-man discourse; so great a character, so much and so great an Englishman.

I saw him a number of times after I graduated, right down to 1955. It was always the same pleasure and I am only sorry I was not able to accept his ever-ready hospitality as often as he offered it. One especially vivid memory remains. During a wartime air raid over Oxford, I begged a night's sleep in his rooms. His scout made me up a wonderful bed on his study floor and while he was doing so, Lewis said to me, "You're a sergeant, I see. I'll bet you terrify them . . . ."

"I don't know about that," said I, "but at all events I'm just about to become a warrant officer. How do you think I shall be then?"

"I think," said Lewis, "you'll be a perfect bastard."

— 5 —

C.S. Lewis, the Teacher

E.L. Edmonds

Professor Edmonds, a pre-war pupil of Lewis's, has written twelve books. A volume of his poetry was published for the International Poetry Society in 1979. He is a Fellow of the Royal Historical Society, of the Royal Society of Arts, and of the English Speaking Board. He has been president of the World Council for Curriculum and Instruction and chairman of the English Speaking Board. He is Professor of Education at the University of Prince Edward Island, Charlottetown. "The main thing," says Professor Edmonds, "is to pay tribute to this great teacher, 'all passion spent.' It would be his wish:

'Speak of me as I am; nothing extenuate
Nor set down aught in malice . . . .' "

Ic tō sōþe wāt
þæt biþ in eorle   indryhten þēaw,
þæt hē his ferðlocan   fæste binde,
healde[1] his hordcofan,   hycge swā hē wille.
(The Wanderer)
(Translation: I know truly that it is an excellent custom for a man to bind fast the promptings of his heart, to keep to himself his innermost thoughts, let him think what he will.)

Prolegomena

Our school hymn was:

> *Forty years on when afar and asunder*
> *Parted are those who are singing today . . . .*

Perhaps, therefore, this is a convenient time for me to open the word-hoard of memory on C.S. Lewis, as it is about that time since my eighth term of tutorials with him had come and gone.

Oxford in the Mid-1930s

It would be impossible to describe Lewis without first putting him into the whole context of Oxford at the time. Here gathered together were so many princes of the academic realm in Britain; and it did not take long for one to realize the majesty of their scholarship. There was, for instance, Gilbert Murray giving a course of lectures on Greek poetry (I still have an affectionate memory of this rosy-cheeked octogenarian piping his dithyrambs). There was the beaming, silver-haired Sir Michael Sadler with a long and distinguished record behind him, both in the field of scholarship and of public administration. Then too there were A.D. Lindsay and John Maud, scholars both who were destined to excel later in similar fields. Nevill Coghill was on the bubble, already doing great things in the world of Shakespearean drama. If we used Ridley's edition of Shakespeare, we had Ridley himself to lecture to us. Then somewhere in the linguistic wings there were the highly idiosyncratic C.L. Wrenn, bullet-headed H.C. Wyld, J.R.R. Tolkien, Horatian "urbanity" personified. Then of course there was Lewis himself.

The mid-thirties were turbulent years and Oxford was as sharply divided over the war in Spain as it was later to be over the war in Katanga (or so I am told). We all had an inkling (!) that war was coming sooner or later—reinforced I recall by a somber lecture by Herr Brüning, former Chancellor of the Weimar Republic. But there was still a tremendous activity in the literary field. I remember receiving, as a college prize, a copy of *The Hobbit,* which had just been published: we all knew that more fabling was to follow. Yet though we might say that "great spirits now on earth are sojourning," their scholarship was carried lightly. I recall Sir Michael Sadler inviting us in to give our opinions on his magnificent collection of surrealist paintings. We manfully staggered through the usual abracadabra of comment about texture, color, composition, etc. He then cheerfully announced that he had hung them all upside down for our benefit (enjoyment even then was the keynote of the lesson!). Perhaps we managed to pass on some of this zest: I seem to remember that we had a visit from Joseph Stalin and we all sang "Poor Old Joe" when he was coming down the steps. (*O si sic omnes!*)

The Oxford Tutorial System

Our own Canadian semester system is so very different from the practice in Oxford that a word of explanation may be timely. Ours was a trimester system (which of course still applies in British universities today). To get into Oxford, we had first to matriculate, and this included taking Latin. In our first term we were expected to take what were called "P. Mods." (Pass Moderations). Four areas of individual study were chosen, (mine were English History, English Literature, Greek Literature, French Literature). Usually at the end of the first term, though the examination could be put off until the end of the second term, we duly wrote a number of qualifying three-hour papers. If successful, we then moved on to whatever Honors Degree course we cared to choose.

So it was that for some two and a half years thereafter, I strode through the cloisters in Magdalen [College], toddled up a certain staircase, knocked on a certain oak door on the left, was welcomed in by a big, booming voice, wafted into an easy chair beside the fire, and thereafter subjected to a "laying bare of the soul" exercise for an academic hour.

The routine was familiar enough. One's allotted tutor generally suggested a reading list of a few books to the student, who faithfully read as many of them as he wished (and more if he were wise!). Having suitably gestated for a week as much as he could, he then produced an essay for the tutor which was read aloud to him. The tutor would then make a few suggestions, raise points for discussion; and ten minutes before the close of the hour, the student would be given a fresh topic, or author, or group of authors, with a new suggested reading list, which of course, in Lewis's case, always included a close and copious study of the texts.

At the beginning of each semester, "collections," (written examinations) were set, based upon the work of the previous term. Then of course at the end of three years, there was a final examination, comprising some twelve or more papers of three hours each. Depending upon how well the student stood up to this physical, as well as mental endurance test, he was awarded an appropriate degree.

Tutorials With C.S. Lewis

The easy chair on the left-hand side of his fireplace, usually reserved for the student, was certainly the largest I have ever seen. I well remember sitting perched on the end of it (it says something perhaps for my own background that I found it impossible to sit back in the armchair and read an essay at the same time. Lewis's own ritual rarely changed. He would first scrutinize his vast array of pipes, some short, some long: one of them was an old churchwarden type of pipe, white with a long stem, of the kind familiar from the painting of the Wellers at the table in the yard of the hostelry. Lewis usually chose a short, curvy-stemmed, chubby, rosewood one. He delved into his pouch of tobacco, or more rarely a tin ("Three Nuns," he once archly told me), thumbed into place a nicely rounded wad, lighted up with a blue cloudy flourish, reclined back in his own easy chair on the right of the fire, and motioned me to begin. While I read, he puffed away steadily at his pipe; and I should add that Lewis was no dilettante with his pipe. He loved a good cloud, including from time to time a few smoke rings of varied convolutions.

I would read my essay, usually something of the order of about twenty pages or so, during which time Lewis would say very little. At the end of my reading, there would be a significant pause. He would then ask one or two questions, usually requiring further elaboration of particular points I had made. We then got into discussion, with Lewis sometimes suggesting at intervals that I might care to read what so-and-so had said on this, etc.

Lewis made no concessions; and perhaps for the first time I learned to submit to criticism. But, he was never cynical or sarcastic; and his own frequent change of intellectual stance taught me one very valuable lesson, namely that no one should be regarded as an absolute authority. Thus, much as he obviously respected Tillyard, Tillyard for him was not the only authority on Milton, anymore than A.C. Bradley's views on Shakespeare were the gospel ones. Indeed, sometimes in argument he would lend a helping hand if I showed signs of giving in too soon (as I am afraid I frequently did). He had a great respect for reading round and I soon acquired the habit from him. I remember his expressing some astonishment that I should know the name of two lakes over which the Geats portaged their ships (Lakes Vanern and Vattern).

He was generous too and would acknowledge any little scraps of knowledge which I had acquired in my previous eighteen years. Thus, I remember his expressing pleasurable surprise when I praised the fables of George MacDonald. He was fascinated that I had met Beatrix Potter[1] and was interested to know how I came to meet her. When we came across the line in *Sir Gawayn and the Green Knight,*

Pe kay fot on pe fold he before sette

I happened to know that "kay" (old Danish *Kei*) was still preserved in various forms (eight in all) in the Yorkshire dialect. He was fascinated to learn what a "kaggy"[2] batsman was. In the same text "misy" also still existed in Lancashire dialect in the form of "mizzy"[3]; and again he expressed great interest. Indeed, I think it was this particular interest that led him to suggest that I go to some tutorials with C.L. Wrenn. Tutorials with this outstanding philologist were memorable encounters.

Lewis's approach to English Literature was strictly chronolological. We started with Anglo-Saxon and finished at 1832. We began with the easier Anglo-Saxon prose, e.g. *The Voyages of Ohthere and Wulfstan* and through the Saxon Chronicle to the fiery, more polemical prose of the sermon of Bishop Wulfstan, Archbishop of York, 1002-1023. We also "did" a considerable number of the poems, including "The Fall of the Angels," "The Seafarer," "Judith," "The Phoenix," and "The Battle of Maldon," (in retrospect, so reminiscent of the Battle of Dunkirk).

Lewis had the happy knack of setting students at their ease very early on ("Don't call me sir, Edmonds, I'm not a sir!"). I like to think he had a photographic memory, for certainly on one of the rare occasions I met him after leaving Oxford, he recalled an essay I had written in praise of William Cowper's hymns. He, himself, I recall, was far less enthusiastic about them. This prompts the thought that it was Lewis who first taught me the importance of one's own experience. When I went up to the university, I "larded the lean earth" with information out of books. Lewis, in fact, said I carried into the examination far too much knowledge, adding that there it may not have been an advantage, though it would be later (I like to think he was right). But, he would regularly elicit *my* opinions on things, quite apart from that of the recognized authorities. He, in turn, set the example. Thus, I had written a fierce condemnation of Dean Swift, commenting on what I considered his unnecessary vulgarity. I had even gone so far as to indicate in *Gulliver's Travels,* Books 3 and 4, the first signs of depravity and Swift's *"saeva indignatio"* which would bring him to the very brink of madness. Lewis grunted, "Have you ever been in an officers' mess, Edmonds? Men talk like that you know." I was soon to discover the truth of that remark. Lewis, we know, had war service and had been wounded in action.

As I got to know Lewis, I could tentatively volunteer information about "extracurricular activities" I might be engaged in. He was always interested to hear about the Martlets Society (of which I was a member*). On another occasion I had gone to see *The Student Prince* and had been carried away by the songs and indeed by the whole way of life which *The Student Prince* represented. I began one tutorial by talking in some detail about this. He looked across at me over the rims of his glasses, as he had a habit of doing, and said, "Hmmm, so you enjoyed it, did you?" He volunteered no further comment, nor did I need one. The message was loud and clear that it wasn't quite up to literary snuff, so to speak.

Once, arising out of our discussion of Milton's sonorous orotund, I said I was singing tenor in the Music Society. He asked, "Have you ever sung counter tenor?"

I gave him the stock answer by anyone who doesn't know what that means, namely, "Well, I'm not sure, really." I certainly had a very high register, so I suppose his question was reasonable. The College Music Society set itself very high standards and I still remember some of the (inevitably literary) pieces we sang, such as "Blest Pair of Sirens" and "My Soul, There Is a Country Far Beyond the Stars." Anyway, Lewis showed me his magnificent record player which had a long, tubular horn

---

* Lewis was also a member.

interfaced with green felt. He played a piece of music which included the refrain, "Make Straight the Way of the Lord," (since identified, I may say, as coming from Orlando Gibbon's "This Is the Record of John"). In a rare moment, he also explained what bourdon was by playing a little bit of Allegri's "Miserere," (51st Psalm). Lewis must have had a good musical background for I still remember it was he who explained what a cadence might mean by referring to Milton's line:

Soft silken primrose fading timelessly.

I have already mentioned how Lewis insisted upon knowing thoroughly the text of the author under discussion. Everyone, for example, is familiar with "Lycidas." But we studied also "Epitaphium Damonis," and I well remember the young romantic Milton first brought before my eyes in the quotation:

> *quis me lenire docebit*
> *Mordaces curas, quis longam fallere noctem*
> *Dulcibus alloquiis, grato cum sibilat igni*
> *Molle pirum, et nucibus strepitat focus, at malus Auster*
> *Miscet cuncta foris, et desuper intonat ulmo?*

> (*Translation: Who shall teach me to assuage the carking cares, who teach me to pass the long night in sweet conversation, while the soft pear hisses on the gentle fire and the hearth crackles with nuts, but the wicked south wind stirs everything up outside and roars down the elm?*)

Lectures by Lewis

These were a joy! Lewis throve on large audiences (his own love of strong verbs will be here apparent!). He did not do too many, as I recall, and the series I best remember were "Prolegomena to Mediaeval Literature." Strangely enough, I don't remember much about the literature, but I do recall how he talked at length about such literary devices as circumlocutio and expositio. He loved to "expatiate and confer" about medieval cosmology, including the "three times three" hierarchy of angels. I still vividly recall his references to the Zodiac, in particular to the cosmetology [sic!]. Lewis, with his pink-and-white complexion and his jovial disposition must surely have been born under Jupiter.

It was in this series of lectures that he emphasized the importance of medieval order. He alluded to the crucial importance of Lady Macbeth's request, "Stand not on the order of your going": the importance of that line, as a clue to the disintegration of Macbeth's power, has stayed with me ever since. Tolkien too loved order and such things that went with it as precedence and all the panoply of array (examples abound in the *Lord of the Rings*).

Incidentally, it was when he was giving this particular series of lectures that he cavalierly referred to all the young women students who inevitably filled the front rows when he was lecturing. He asked them if they had their pens at the ready, on one occasion, and as a young male chauvinist at the time, I joined in the laughter. If Lewis had any women students for tutorials, I cannot say: certainly I never saw any (more's the pity!).

The Beowulf Soirees

On selected evenings, Lewis would gather around him a small group of his students who met in his room to read *Beowulf* aloud and to discuss particular textual, grammatical, or historical points. I should add that this was not "swot." The part of *Beowulf* we read was not the part that was set for examination purposes. We could bring our own beer mugs if we liked, but he had a goodly selection of his own in case we preferred to use his—as we usually did. We drank his beer with gusto (this is still a function of youth presumably?) but I do recall having read Tacitus's account of the Chatti in the Germania; and it was attractively easy to fall into chanting, which the Chatti loved to do; as do their descendants today, when they foregather for their powerful group singing!

I remember these *Beowulf* readings with great affection. I came to know that there were one or two other students of Lewis who were about the same business as I was, and we could exchange points of view. Lewis encourged such discussion, but he also encouraged any inclination to wander into the byways and sideways of Anglo-Saxon literature. I can still vividly remember one animated discussion about damascening of swords. The *Beowulf* line was in reference to Naegling:

> *ecg waes īrēn   ātertānum fah.*

At(t)or certainly could mean poison—a reference in *Aelfric's Homilies* confirmed that; and I thought there could be a possible echo of "atorcoppe," suggestive of spiders and poison. Against this, however, was the whole weight of tradition, actual or assumed, that the heroes of *Beowulf* would never fight with poisoned swords. Lewis had a sword, a regimental one I would imagine it was—and he showed us some of the wavy damascened lines, both on the blade and on the hilt (no runes, alas!).

The study of etymology of words may be out of fashion today, but Lewis insisted on it. He picked up Tyndale's use of "scapegoat" (in his translation of the New Testament from the Greek in 1525). Milton's coinages, "pandemonium" or "ethereal," for example, received close attention. We noted Milton's strikingly transitive use of the verb "scowl" in "scowls o'er the darkened landscape snow and showers." His reference to "charm of earliest birds" took us back to Anglo-Saxon "*cyrm*"; to the "charms" too, which we had already studied, as well as to other later usages, by Sir Walter Scott, for instance. Lewis also liked the finer points of grammar: I recall his pointing out to me the distinction between "due to" and "owing to." For some reason I also associate Lewis with a discussion on ethic datives in Shakespeare. But he was no arid grammarian. He once encouraged me to write a play about life in a mining village. That it was never finished was my own fault. Time just ran out.

Lewis and Tolkien

It was at the *Beowulf* soirées that I first came under the spell of J.R.R. Tolkien. He was Rawlinson and Bosworth Professor of Anglo-Saxon at the time, and came in quite often. It was very obvious that the two of them were great friends—indeed, they were like two young bear cubs sometimes, just happily quipping with one another. I have a hunch (and I have refused to check to find out, in case the illusion is lost) that both Lewis and Tolkien went to public (boarding) schools at some period in their early years. Certainly they must have gone to boys' schools only. I say this because such a type of single-sex schooling has always seemed to me to develop a kind of adolescent idealism which is carried over into adulthood—a continuing attachment to a boyish,

"Greyfriars," code of loyalty to each other.[4] I have often thought it is one reason why the knights of King Arthur to Lewis, and the heroes of the sagas to Tolkien, were so attractive. If I am right, I would go further and suggest that it was this commonality of background in both men, either acquired or instinctively assumed, that predisposed both of them to the art of fabling, where good and evil can always be suitably anthropomorphized. I still remember Lewis suggesting that no one was so good at hinting evil as Beatrix Potter (Mr. Piperson, in the *Tale of Pigling Bland,* was mentioned). Tolkien also had some pretty good descriptions of monsters (prototype Balrogs and the like). Both Tolkien and Lewis were interested in riddling. Indeed, we did quite a number of the Anglo-Saxon riddles with Lewis, and he threw in one or two of his own from time to time (*pace* Bilbo and Gollum!).

Tolkien it was who reinterpreted the spirit of *Beowulf* for us into Icelandic terms. Thus, Beowulf replies to Hrothgar's lament:

> ' Ne sorga, snotor guma!   Sēlre bið æghwǣm,
> þæt hē his frēond wrece,   þonne hē fela murne.
> Ūre æghwylc sceal   ende gebīdan
> worolde līfes;   wyrce sē þe mōte
> dōmes ǣr dēaþe;   þæt bið drihtguman
> unlifgendum   æfter sēlest.,

> (*Translation: Do not grieve, O wise warrior. Better it is for every man to avenge his friend rather than greatly mourn. Each of us must needs await the end of life in the world. Let him who can achieve a reputation before he dies. That is best for a noble warrior when life is over.*)

And so Havamal, Verse 77, terse, laconic, gnomic:

> Deyr fe   Deyja fraendr
> Deyr sjalfr   it sama;
> Ek veit eina   Si aldri deyr;
> Domr um dauoan hvern.

> (*Translation: Cattle die, kinsmen die, and so each one of us will die; I know one thing that never dies: the repute of every dead man.*)

One other thing I could not fail to remember about Tolkien and Lewis when they were together; apart from their shaggy tweeds. This was their inveterate habit of playing at smoke rings. Sometimes, each would try for the best sequence of rings, and it is still a source of wonderment to me how they managed to send up one ring and then put two or three more rings through very quickly before the first ring dissipated. Of such smoking habits were those of Gandalf formed?

Lewis, the Teacher, in Retrospect

Carl Rogers says in *Being Himself with Others*:

> *The quality of the personal encounter is probably, in the long run, the element which determines the extent to which this is an experience which releases or promotes development and growth. I believe the quality of my encounter is more important in the long run than my scholarly knowledge, my professional training, my counseling orientation, the techniques I use.*

I have thought long about this, as I have about another quotation from J.G. Fitch; it says that we teach not so much by what we know as by what we are. Obviously Lewis had a tremendous effect upon me as upon anyone with whom he came into a relationship, such as the Oxford Tutorial System generated. Here was this craggy man, with a deep belly laugh, "broad as ten thousand beeves at pasture," with no mean dewlap of his own as he sat: a jolly farmer to look at, yet with all the sensitivity to mood and word of the author of *The Wanderer* or *The Dream of the Rood*. Always he was probing, always testing to see how far a particular student could go. He once handed me Owen Barfield's book called *Poetic Diction* and asked me to read and comment on it. The essay I wrote was an unmitigated disaster so far as I was concerned (and, indeed, so far as he was concerned too). But, he loved to throw out challenges and see if a student would pick them up. It was this aura of learning which he carried about with him as consistently as the scent of tobacco on his sports coat. Thus, Renaissance Italy was, for me, eons of light years away. I remember his saying one day, "Well, Edmonds, why don't you read Tasso's *Gerusalemme Liberata*?"

I said that I had no Italian, whereupon he recommended

Elizabethan Edward Fairfax's translation (under the title of *Godfrey de Bulloigne*). It was a splendid interlinear exercise, but an even more splendid experience, extending to such other "realms of gold" as Chapman's *Homer;* Pope's *Iliad;* and Cecil Day Lewis's *Aeneid.*

The polymathic nature of Lewis's scholarship was always in evidence. It was something that Oxford had been very good at inculcating in its students. If one looks, for example, at Her Majesty's Inspectors of Schools in the nineteenth century, many of them came from Oxford or Cambridge and nearly all of them had this ability to move with ease in several disciplines. Much the same could be said of the political figures sired by Oxford and Cambridge. It was Lewis who introduced me to the idea, well put by Walter de la Mare that:

> *Our master words, symbols for all that is near and dear, for all that we dislike or despise, are richly autobiographical. Our very selves are bound up with them. Memories and emotions cluster about them like the tiny sprigs of seaweed and the minute living anemones on the shell of a hermit crab. They are in the service of our solitude as well as of our intercourse.*

Though, as I've said, English literature for me stopped at 1832, Lewis gave me an in-depth love of Anglo-Saxon literature; a "romantic passion" for Arthurian legend, including the *Red Book of Hergest* (not unknown to Tolkien, either); a great love of Spenser and Milton; an even greater love of Wordsworth. Of the "devil dodging," razor-sharp Christian apologist, I saw little: certainly he did not appear to us in that role at the time. For the true Christian exegesis, we went to St. Mary's Church where the Sunday evening sermons, organized by the then Canon Cockin, provided some of the finest intellectual exercises in Christianity one could ever wish to hear. One by William Temple (then Archbishop of York) was particularly memorable. *The Pilgrim's Regress,* (1933) may have given some hint of what was to come from Lewis: but for us neophytes, he was the author of the *Allegory of Love* (1936)—and the seeming, sublimated frustrations of the tradition of courtly love.

Along with Lewis's scholarship went order and precision. I had a turgid style and he constantly urged me to simplify it. He was a tiger where spelling and quotation were concerned. Even a slight mis-quotation, he said, was an insult to the author and an affront to him. He might well have been a literary Strafford, with his motto of thoroughness!

Conclusion

In all this talk today about the teacher being a facilitator, a counselor, a resource person, etc., I think we are in great danger of forgetting one other important attribute, probably more important than all the rest put together, namely, the tang of the teacher. Forty years on, I ask myself what would be a fair definition of the purposes of education as propounded by Lewis. I go back to a definition by William Johnson Cory, Master at Eton, in 1875:

> *In school you are not engaged so much in acquiring knowledge as in making mental efforts under criticism. A certain amount of knowledge you can indeed, with average facilities, acquire so as to retain, nor need you regret the hours you spend on much that is forgotten, for the shadow of lost knowledge at least protects you from many illusions. But you go to a great school not so much for knowledge as for arts and habits; for the habit of attention, for the art of expression, for the art of assuming at a moment's notice a new intellectual position, for the habit of submitting to censure and refutation, for the art of indicating assent or dissent in graduated terms, for the art of working out what is possible in a given time, for discrimination, for mental courage and mental sobriety.*

Important as the modern affective approach may be of simply "helping students to be themselves," I think we neglect at our peril the refining influence of sustained disciplining of the mind. This applies equally to the teacher. "No lamp can light another unless it burns its own flame:" a comment by Rabindranath Tagore, perfectly exemplified by Lewis throughout a lifetime.

Looking back, I ask myself what valediction Lewis might have pronounced on the annual generation of departing students. He would probably have looked over his eyebrows, as was his wont, and quoted from his beloved *Divine Comedy*:

> *Non aspettar mio dir piu, ne mio cenno.*
> *Libero, dritto e sano e tuo arbitrio,*
> *E fallo fora non fare a suo senno;*
> *Per ch' io te sopra te corono e mitrio.'*

> *(Translation: No more expect my word nor my sign. Free,*
> *upright and whole is thy will, and 'twere a fault not to act*
> *according to its prompting; wherefore I do crown and mitre*
> *thee over thyself.)*

The master indeed of them that know![5]

A Personal Postscript

Yet in one respect, Lewis may have misled me and possibly others too. Some years later, I was to "go through the valley of the shadow of death" as Lewis did with his Joy. But at the very end, she was in the hospital and under sedation: his experience therefore was not mine at home on the banks of my Ruth's beloved Clyde:

To My Old Tutor, C.S. Lewis

> *Do you recall, Sir,*
> *Those days gone by*
> *Uncertain glory*
> *When very much* in statu pupilari
> *We downed your nut-brown ale*
> *From Toby jugs and pewter mugs*
> *Declaiming* Beowulf *and Finnsburg's tale*
> *Or gentle Spenser's deeds of derring-do*
> *Through smoke-rings blue.*

> *You spoke with high degree of certainty.*

> *In later years, Sir,*
> *I read your mind*
> *Your grief observed*
> *Both fear and faith entwined.*
> *With Dante you opined*

She smiled, and then inclined
Toward a lasting fire
Ethereal desire.
"Sorrise e riguardommi;
Poi si torno all'eterna fontana."

You wrote so very reassuringly.

But now, Sir
I have to say
Your words go like the wind.
There was no dignity
Spiritual reconciliation
But only agony
Shared mutually

Finally
Humiliation
Slow disintegration.
So grievously awry
Your allegory.

Helpless I saw her beauty die
Irrecoverably
While faith nearby
Hovered—reluctantly.

Nevertheless, I think it significant that in an hour of crisis I should have
turned to this great teacher to expiate and to sublimate my own grief.

— 6 —

Part A: With Girls at Home

Patricia Heidelberger

Mrs. Patricia (Boshell) Heidelberger, as a young girl in England during the first year of the war, was moved around from house to house and had never been able to settle happily with various "foster" parents, most of whom had a background and life style very different from her own. Then in September, 1940, she went to live at the Kilns, the Lewis's home in Headington, near Oxford. The following account is actually part of a letter from Mrs. Heidelberger to Dr. Clyde Kilby, both of whom kindly consent to its publication. Mrs. Heidelberger now lives in California.

The Kilns! Coming to that gracious home with its garden, lake, tennis court and the hens—oh, those hens!—was like moving out of the shadows into the sunlight. Since that time I have read much about Mrs. Moore's authoritativeness,[1] her short temper and selfishness; but with us she was kind, solicitous, and indeed, most forbearing. The eternal cigarette hanging on her lower lip didn't worry us in the least, except that we suspected that as often as not, it dripped into our food.

My first impression of C.S. Lewis was that of a shabbily clad, rather portly gentleman, whom I took to be the gardener, and told him so. He roared—boomed!—with laughter. And then with a twinkle in his eye, he said, "Welcome, girls." What characterized him most was his tolerance. "Microbe,"—Marie José Bosc, my co-evacuee—and I were extremely lively, noisy and giggly. He never reproached us. Fortunately, we were also both quite studious, and during the next year, when both of us were preparing to take school-leaving certificate, he would invite us many an evening into his smoke-laden den, go through our homework with us and impart ideas. Once I had to write an essay on the theater. I was struggling over a suitable end phrase to round up my opus. Lewis suggested: "We are such stuff as dreams are made of." It was just right: and I won a prize for that essay. When, later, I told him I wanted to go up to Oxford (University), he encouraged me, coached me in Latin, and even taught me a little Greek.

And how generous he was! When my mother, a widow, came to visit shortly before I sat for my entrance exam, Lewis made her an offer of financial assistance towards paying my university dues. His only stipulation was that it should be kept secret. My mother accepted; and thus it is largely due to his generosity that I was able to graduate, and later, take my master's degree. It is my understanding that he similarly helped "Microbe" when she went on to train as a nurse.

I was saddened to hear that his brother, Major Lewis, had died. I corresponded with him at the time of C.S. Lewis's death. As schoolgirls, we didn't have a great deal of rapport with him, though he was always friendly. I would describe him as "avuncular" towards us.

In all, I look back on those years as two of the happiest of my school life. Unlike most evacuees, we were comfortable, we were well fed—I grew fat!—and we seemed to be loved. I enjoyed the scholarly sessions in the den; I borrowed books; I learned about Tolkien and the Inklings. I think "Microbe" and I were extremely fortunate, and more than a little spoiled.

Part B: With Girls at Home

Jill Freud

> *Mrs. Clement (Jill) Freud lived at the Kilns later in the war. It had originally been arranged that she should be billeted with the family. Mrs. Moore invited Jill, aged sixteen, to stay at the Kilns for a holiday. She stayed for the summer of 1943, helping with the house, shopping and animals. When the time came for Jill to begin her training for the stage, Mrs. Moore was ill and the family was without any other help. So Jill stayed for two years. I met Jill, now Mrs. Freud, on holiday in a small place called Walberswick, on the west coast of Suffolk. She is a busy mother of five children, and a keen horsewoman. Occasionally, she acts. She was studying for her part in William Douglas Home's play, "The Dame of Sark." Her husband Clement Freud, the well-known broadcaster, writer, and member of Parliament, is a grandson of Sigmund Freud, the famous founder of psychoanalysis. The following account is by Mrs. Freud.*

The following quotes are taken from *Brothers and Friends: The Diaries of Major Warren Hamilton Lewis,* edited by Clyde S. Kilby and Marjorie Lamp Mead, (Harper and Row, San Francisco, 1982). We are grateful to the publishers for their permission to use this material.

"Our dear, delightful June Flewett (Jill Flewett Freud) leaves us tomorrow, after nearly two years, for London and the Dramatic School where she is to be taught to be an actress. She is not yet eighteen, but I have met no one of any age further advanced in the Christian way of life. From seven in the morning till nine at night, shut off from people of her own age, almost grudged the time for her religious duties, she has slaved at the Kilns, for a fraction of an hour; I have never seen her other than gay, eager to anticipate exigent demands, never complaining, always self-accusing in the frequent crises of that dreary house. Her reaction to the meanest ingratitude was to seek its cause in her own faults. She is one of those rare people to whom one can venture to apply the word 'saintly.' . . .From a personal, selfish point of view I shall feel the loss of June very keenly: for in addition to her other virtues, she is a clever girl, and with her gone, it means that when J [C.S. Lewis] is away, there is no one to talk to in the house." (Tuesday, 2 January 1945) pp. 180-181.

"We—Mollie and Len Miller and myself—got back yesterday afternoon from a capital holiday in June [Flewett Freud]'s seaside 'cottage' at Walberswick over in Suffolk, she with her unfailing kindness having lent it to me for a fortnight . . . ." (Friday, 27 May 1966) p. 259.

We had twenty-five hens and thirty rabbits in hutches in a large garden. Mrs. Moore was a frail, old woman in her seventies, and ill with varicose ulcers. I fed the hens and rabbits and cleaned the coops and helped with the housework. There was Paxford, the gardener, and Miss Morris, who lived in a bungalow in the garden. Altogether there were about half a dozen of us in the household. I gathered up the eggs every day. We ate most of them. The others were preserved in water glass. I went to London to take entrance examinations to the Royal Academy of Dramatic Art. But the time I was accepted Miss Morris had left and Mrs. Moore was worse. Of course Lewis was teaching at Magdalen every day.

I didn't know who he was at first. I knew C.S. Lewis was the most famous man in Oxford. Everyone knew that. I had read some of his books. But I didn't know he was the "Jack" Lewis to whom I was introduced at the Kilns. Mrs. Moore and Warnie called him Jack. I called him Jack. He was very easy and pleasant to talk to, and I talked to him freely about myself and my opinions: I would have been embarrassed if I had known he was C.S. Lewis. When I did learn who he was, I was shocked. He had such a great understanding of human nature that I felt he must have known my every thought.

You can imagine that the day-to-day conversation of a man with a first-class brain and a tremendous education, a teacher whose mind was on literature, theology, and critical arguments—that such conversation was on a much higher level than I had ever participated in before. Just to sit quietly and listen was an education.

Almost every Sunday night the brothers listened to a complete symphony on Major Lewis's old gramophone. It had a large, wooden, handmade horn. The sound was good and he was proud of it; no one else was allowed to use it. But what Jack Lewis imposed—I should say unwittingly and continually impressed on me—were ideas and books. Most of the talk at meals was literary. Indeed we were always talking about books. He would lend me various volumes. And he told me to go to Blackwell's Bookshop in Oxford, anytime, and buy any book I wanted on his account. I did once. I was too shy to go again. But living with Lewis was like having one's own private tutor.

I noticed some of the things that have been written about Lewis, comments by people who have been taught by him, in his biography and elsewhere. Some give the impression that he would perhaps make them feel intellectually inferior: and obviously there has been a certain amount of resentment about this. May I say I went to the Kilns with no opinion whatever of my intellectual ability. Lewis was the first person who made me believe that I was an intelligent human being and the whole of the time I was there he built up my confidence in myself and in my ability to think and understand. He never put me down. He never made me feel foolish, no matter how small my contribution towards any conversation might be. If he thought I was particularly silly the most he would do would be just to refrain from answering. He might perhaps ignore something I had said. I left the Kilns with deeper understanding, and with a belief that I was of value.

Major Warnie Lewis was the same. He was by nature a gentler, less demanding person, and less stimulating. He was comfy to be with all the time and obviously highly intelligent. But he was not looking for an intellectual response from you in the same way that Jack Lewis did. But I also realize—after reading what other people have said—that the very kindness of approach Jack Lewis had towards me was because I was not as intelligent as his undergraduates. He would have been tougher with me if I could have taken it. How very ill-equipped I was to deal with him! And he was so kind! Over the years, it is a compliment that has reversed itself but I can accept it now. If he had let me see how ignorant I was at the time, I would have suffered from it. But now I can look back and see what he did for me. He built up my self-esteem.

And he did the same for others too. For some months we had a young man living at the Kilns. He worked as a houseboy and general helper. He was probably introduced by the Social Services Department, and he was what we would now call educationally subnormal. He had the mentality of a child of eight. Every evening Jack Lewis taught him to read. Lewis made drawings and letter cards for him; he went through the alphabet with him and tried to teach him small words, and so on. I don't think he had a great deal of success because the young man found it hard to retain anything. But for more than two months Jack Lewis went through the alphabet with him every evening.

To Mrs. Moore, Lewis showed the greatest loving care. He waited on her, filled her hot water bottle, made her a hot drink, saw that she was tucked in each night. The only time I ever heard Jack Lewis's voice rise in annoyance with her was once when she had said something derogatory about his brother. She was strong-willed, and had a great sense of humor. Mrs. Moore and Jack Lewis had happy times together. She adored him absolutely. Her whole life was centered around him and around him alone. The running of the house, the cooking, the meals—everything she did—was geared for Jack's happiness and comfort. The whole household revolved on the premise that Jack must be looked after, and Warnie was expected to tag along. I am sure she restricted Jack's life tremendously but she did give everything of herself to him that she could. When she became ill she took all Jack's letters, piles of letters she had received from him over a period of about twenty-five years, and I think also the letters from her son, Paddy—Lewis's great friend who was killed in the First World War—and threw them all into the old-fashioned boiler in the kitchen. She burned the lot.

When I had married after the war, my husband and I stayed at the Kilns once; and later we took our children once or twice. Over the years we went there a few times. Many years later, when I had not seen or heard much from the Lewises for quite a long time, not since Jack had himself married, I wrote and asked if I could come and see them. It was arranged. I was to go there for dinner in a few days. But Jack had not been well and the night President Kennedy was assassinated I rang the Kilns to say I was coming. I actually telephoned within half an hour of Jack's death. I spoke to Warnie. Of course he was in a very shocked condition and told me Jack was dead. It was a terrible night.

I had a bundle of wonderful letters from Jack. When I moved from one house to another, alas, they were lost. He called me June, actually Juin. When he wrote he always began, "Dear Juin." I can't remember why. He gave me a copy of the *Screwtape Letters,* and in the front he wrote,

> *Beauty and brains and virtue never dwell*
> *Together in one place, the critics say.*
> *Yet we have known a case*
> *You must not ask her name*
> *But seek it 'twixt July and May.*

— 7 —

Part A: With Women at College

Rosamund Cowan

*Mrs. Cowan is one of the very few women who were
tutored by Lewis at Oxford. A curious coincidence led me to
her.*

Undoubtedly one of Lewis's favorite books was the
Iliad. *How often he read it is a matter for conjecture. His
friend Owen Barfield told me he and Lewis used to read and
translate it to each other, taking turns of twenty lines.[1] Only
a few weeks before Lewis died he read it again and wrote to
another friend that he had never enjoyed it more.[2]*

*In an old manor in Stanton Harcourt, a small village in
Oxfordshire, Pope toiled for some years to produce (with
much help) a translation of the* Iliad. *This translation, one
of several, is generally considered to be the most famous—
but not by Lewis. He does not even consider it a translation;
he considers it a parody.[3]*

Now the point about the Iliad *that interests me is that
"human nature has not materially altered in the three
thousand years since Homer wrote," as Mr. E.V. Rieu
remarks in the introduction to his current prose translation.[4] I enjoyed this book so much I wrote to Mr. Rieu; and
I must have mentioned something about Lewis because
Mr. Rieu replied that he "had the pleasure of meeting C.S.
Lewis once or twice." A few years after reading Mr. Rieu's
translation of the* Odyssey, *I wrote again for the same*

reason. Alas, he had died. A reply came from his daughter, Rosamund, who said that as a war-time student of St. Hugh's College, Oxford, she had been a pupil of Lewis's. A lucky break for me! She is now a Mrs. Cowan. Her husband is a physician. I interviewed her at their home in Hertfordshire.

It was a joy to study with Lewis. He treated us like queens. I think Pat Thomson and I were the first women students he had. He had perfect manners, always standing up when we came in. And he brought to everything a remarkable original approach. At first we were a bit frightened as he had a reputation of being a "man's man." We rather thought he would be a bit down on women. Actually he was delightful. He told me I reminded him of a Shakespearean heroine—a compliment I've always cherished. He certainly treated me like one.

But, mind you, he stood no nonsense from us. I mean we had to express our *own* opinions, not other people's, and express them clearly and honestly. He didn't want a scholarly, purely intellectual approach. And I can tell you that when it came to reading one's own essay aloud to him one felt decidedly uncomfortable if one had not put something of one's own experience and understanding into it. Then we would talk about it, and criticize, always politely. Tutorials were never dull; he would make them lively.

I was amazed when I heard he had married. He had always been such a confirmed bachelor, completely self-contained. He had his own life, his regular walks, Charles Williams and Owen Barfield; and he didn't seem to need feminine companionship. And he was well looked after at Magdalen. He had beautiful rooms and excellent food and wine. The dons lived well. He had many friends in Oxford; and he was well known and liked.

When I heard his "Broadcast Talks"[5] on the radio I thought they were marvelous. So were his lectures. I was studying literature so I went to his lectures. Not only the English students went. The whole university who were interested in literature at all. Some medical and science people. The political people. Everybody went. If Lewis was known to be lecturing the big hall in Magdalen was absolutely full. They were even sitting on the window sills. He was so good. Wonderful.

He prepared his lectures very carefully and they were more or less written out. He didn't read them. They were so carefully spoken you could take notes. He wanted you to take notes. He quoted and waited while you wrote it down. He lectured on Medieval literature and he gave you the feeling of the period. He made you feel you were right in it. I loved his lectures. I remember he looked very red, with a round face. He was quite ugly, really.

I was in St. Mary's the night he gave his address on "The Weight of Glory." It was marvelous. But you see when I was young at Oxford although I knew he was a remarkable man of exceptional mind, I didn't realize his greatness as you do now. It's always that way, isn't it? I heard him give another talk on miracles.[6] I was so impressed I wrote to him; and he replied on a small scrap of paper, so typical of him.

30 Shepherd's Hill,
Highgate,
London, N.6
Sunday, 27 Sept. 1942

Dear Mr. Lewis,

I knew beforehand that I should be much moved by your address tonight, and I knew from experience that I should sit entranced, but I never dreamed that I should approach remotely near to believing in the subject of your talk.

It would, I fear, be false if I professed to a wholehearted conviction even now, for I don't regard myself as competent to arrive at any such vital decision as yet. But if ever I reached years of such discretion that I could come to that belief to which you so eloquently professed it could surely be on account of no other argument, or rather proof, than that which you brought forward today. If only I had allowed myself to be swept off my feet, to accept what at the time all my reason, all my imagination and all my senses, seemed to warrant, I should without hesitation have pronounced on my return home, "I believe in miracles."

But as it is, when so much of your address was based on the tacit agreement of the main structure of the Christian faith, it would be as absurd for me to believe in an isolated part of it such as miracles, as to believe in the Resurrection if I doubted the Virgin Birth.

I should love to know if you yourself consider that your arguments could in any way apply or be of value if they did not assume Christianity. I mean, if you were not a Christian, would a deep appreciation of the validity, logicality and desirability of those arguments be ground enough on which to base your conversion, or are they only of true value to those who already believe?

Please forgive my disturbing what I hope is the peace of your vacation by writing, but such an address could not but deeply impress your grateful hearers, of whom I am by no means the least impressed nor the least grateful.

Yours sincerely,
Rosamund Rieu.

Dear Mr Lewis,

[handwritten letter, largely illegible]

Yours faithfully,

Rosamund [Cowan]

As from Magdalen, Oxford
Sept. 28th, '42

Dear Miss Rieu,

Speaking in a Church I assumed:

1. Belief in the divinity of Jesus.

2. Belief in the general historicity of the New Testament: and hence,

3. That if *any* miracles *could* be true, these ones would be. My argument only attempted to prove that the existence of the supernatural was certain and its irruption into the Natural Order not improbable. If the argument was valid you could quite logically accept it while reserving judgment on the question whether the New Testament miracles were facts or not, since their particular probability depends on my (1) and (2) which you don't grant. Just as a person might admit *in principle* that a miraculous birth is not an absurdity and yet, if the housemaid has a baby and claims to be a virgin, disbelieve it. Of course, if evidence for the housemaid's virtue and angelic sanctity were overwhelming and if the child turned out to be like no other child—why, then, one would be well-advised to reconsider one's first view and ask the girl's pardon for your misunderstanding.

Yours sincerely,
C.S. Lewis

Part B: With Women at College

Patricia (Thomson) Berry

> *Mrs. Patricia Berry (née Thomson) accompanied Mrs.*
> *Cowan to Lewis's tutorials. "None of us girls was in love*
> *with him," she says. "Indeed he was not handsome. If you'd*
> *put a blue apron round his thick waist, he would have looked*
> *like a benevolent butcher." Mrs. Berry has written/edited*
> *four scholarly books[1] and is now on the staff of London*
> *University. She entitled her contribution* The Academic
> Influence of Lewis.

Before the war, most English grammar schools and high schools
tried to get their sixth-formers into Oxbridge, or failing that, the
University of London. Scotland, Ireland and Wales were different. We
knew that C.H. Herford, the polymath, emanated from Manchester and
J. Dover Wilson, the Shakespearean, from Edinburgh. But that was
pretty well the extent of our knowledge of English honors schools
outside the narrow spheres of Oxbridge and London. Accordingly, with
a head full of books and dreaming spires, I went up to Oxford in 1940. I
think I might have been almost as happy at Cambridge, under the
influence of Basil Willey and F.R. Leavis, with no Old English and
plenty of critical analysis, plus controversies over the value of Milton,
for example. Of the latter I heard little until I took my first academic
post in Sheffield in 1946. To an Oxonian it was incredible that a matter
of literary evaluation should generate such heat. "Oh, these people who
like Milton do annoy me," exclaimed the wife of an eminent professor
on the staff, seeming to suggest that one chose one's friends for their
literary opinions. It was healthy all the same, for I had to rethink all that
Oxford had taught me of *Paradise Lost* and much else. Yet my
admiration for Milton is now unshakable. I also quickly learned to value
our great civic universities.

The Oxford English school in 1940 was dominated by C.S. Lewis.
He was the leading light of the Socratic Club. His lectures, talks and
sermons collected crowds. His tutorials were a stimulus even to those

who disagreed with his judgments. (In any case, he met disagreement with polite, if trenchant, counterattack.) C.S. Lewis could cover practically the whole of Oxford's English syllabus at that time. The only exception was drama, which, Shakespeare apart, he seemed not to care about. Literature after 1820 hardly came into it. Some of us were loud in our laments that we had to pore over *The Anglo-Saxon Chronicle* and *The Owl and the Nightingale* when we wanted to study the Victorians and our own senior contemporaries such as T.S. Eliot (then, as now, a favorite poet of mine). Lord David Cecil did lecture on the Victorian novel, but most of the omitted modernism was left to the thriving English Society. I remember Lewis's mention of George MacDonald and Edith Sitwell, but within the course occasions rarely arose for the discussion of contemporary literature. In retrospect I am glad for that old-fashioned Oxford syllabus. We were expected to be scholars before we could become critics. We would never have discovered the beauties of Old and Middle English poetry for ourselves. These were wonderfully communicated by Lewis, J.R.R. Tolkien and Dorothy Everett. Because of this background, it has been easier to catch up with nineteenth-century and twentieth-century literature later—on one's own.

C.S. Lewis was a man of formidable learning. He had read *Literae Humaniores* before he read English. Thus he could draw on Homer, Virgil and *Beowulf* with equal ease. He was also well versed in Italian and French literature. But all this learning would have been nothing had he not also possessed a Johnsonian power of turning knowledge into wisdom. That makes one momentarily regret that he has had no Boswell to immortalize his *bons mots*. The accounts of him by Owen Barfield, Nevill Coghill and others, however, give valuable insights. But in any case not even the most intimate of his admirers would really put him in Johnson's class.

Before going up to Oxford, students might already have heard of *The Allegory of Love*, still a scholarly classic today. This book is like Bradley's *Shakespearian Tragedy*, Empson's *Seven Types of Ambiguity*, Wilson Knight's *The Wheel of Fire* and Eliot's *Selected Essays*, all of which have turned the tide of scholarly or critical thinking, being quite distinct from the mass of current academic ephemerae. Not that these works close the twentiety-century chapter. Since they were written, Frances Yates's books, for example, have had a similar effect.

Good books demand good readers. The *Allegory of Love* could lead one up the garden path of so-called 'courtly love poetry' and particularly of the component of adultery in it. As for the latter, Lewis knew perfectly well that if Chaucer's Criseyde was not married, his Emily certainly was. It is not fair to distort what he wrote—or to receive it as holy writ. The unpretentious *Preface to Paradise Lost,* published in the early war years, remains a useful, factual guide. *English Literature in the Sixteenth-Century (excluding drama),* appearing after the war, a product of lifelong study, is more controversial. Lewis seems either to deny that the Renaissance occurred or to think it a bad thing if it did. He distinguishes between 'drab' and 'golden' poetry, and though he keeps explaining that 'drab' is not meant to be a derogatory term, it certainly sounds loaded. Perhaps it would have been less misleading had he used the conventional categories, 'plain' and 'aureate,' as usually applied to the fifteenth-century poetry on which so much of the sixteenth depends. It is also amazing that anyone who has read Douglas's and Surrey's translations of the *Aeneid* should prefer the former. But these are like 'the petty cavillings of petty minds.' The pages on Skelton, Sidney, Spenser and Bacon are amongst many brilliant expositions in a book which is itself one of the most brilliant in the O.H.E.L. series.

In 1940 C.S. Lewis had been a Christian for a decade. In his turn, he was instrumental in the conversions of many impressionable young people, by interviews willingly granted, by sermons and by such books as *The Screwtape Letters, The Problem of Pain, Miracles* and *Mere Christianity.* Perhaps his solemn utterances about 'Gawd,' as he termed the Almighty, were a bit embarrassing. But there is little doubt that Christians, agnostics and atheists alike have benefited from his discourses.

Lewis was thought to be a misogynist at that time, enjoying chiefly the company of J.R.R. Tolkien, Charles Williams and other Inklings members, with whom he regularly met. He certainly did complain that the women's colleges of Oxford produced "dull, but meritorious" candidates for the B.A. There is a reference in *Surprised by Joy* to an omitted episode in this autobiography. Possibly it relates to a youthful love affair, though Lewis appeared to have little firsthand knowledge of women, and obviously he had none of marriage. It is impossible to imagine a girl present at his 'Beer with *Beowulf'* evenings in Magdalen.

Many rejoiced at that late, but happy marriage of his. It is a sad paradox that the author of *The Problem of Pain* should, as a despondent widower, write the only book, *A Grief Observed,* that harks back to his former religious scepticism: though he never lost faith in God's existence, He was not always there when wanted. Like the rest, it is a very honest book.

Owing to the call-up of men in World War II, Lewis consented to teach women students. So the scholar in my year at St. Hugh's accompanied me weekly to Magdalen where we had our minds thoroughly spring cleaned. Someone reports that Lewis disliked tutorials. He did not show it. Instead of reminding us, as other tutors had done, of what we had left out of our essays, he considered what was in them. He did not encourage us to bow to his value judgments, but to form our own. His comments for or against our work were just, his conversation highly enlightening to young, would-be intellectuals. His manner to the "ladies of St. Hugh's" was most gracious.

Though Clive Staples Lewis was much admired by all my generation of undergraduates, few of us are likely to welcome a Lewis cult. Anecdotes about his holidays or committee work will not, in the absence of a Boswell, please forever. (I do not mean to say that to date they have been anything but interesting and entertaining.) Goodness knows whether Lewis himself would have enjoyed a periodical in his name.

My own debt to C.S. Lewis is of the kind that can never be repaid except by gratitude. He was for me a good, as well as a great, man, and to have been taught by him has been one of the greatest privileges of my life. Of the thinkers I have encountered since 1940, only R.H. Tawney has affected me in anything like the same way.

Part C: With Women at College

Joan B. Pile

C.S. Lewis was so kind to me at a rather bad time in my life. I was honored to know him as a friend. But I am afraid I destroyed many of his letters when I went to Australia.

Actually I wondered why Mr. Lewis ceased to write to me. I had no idea that he was ill, or that he had died. I had wondered if he had been more hurt than it had appeared he was, when a bad woman had some letters published in the paper, about his correspondence with her; and I did not write again in case it now embarrassed him to keep up our friendship. He was too good and gentlemanly for anyone who knew him to believe such rubbish. A Miss Lewis wrote to me some time ago, asking for information about our friendship, as she wanted to publish a book. But at the time I was very ill and the letter was mislaid by other people.

When I was still comparatively young, I lost my husband, then I developed an illness from which I was told I could not recover. On top of that, I was told my little daughter was likely to be mentally defective. I did not die, and as my son was at a good public school, and my daughter needed a great deal of medical attention, I went to Oxford, to read social science. It was there that I met Mr. Lewis. I suddenly realized that I had left my home and children, and had lost my husband. It all came over me in a rush. Someone mentioned Mr. Lewis to me, and *The Screwtape Letters*. From the book I knew that Mr. Lewis must know almost everything about human beings that it was possible to know. I found that clergymen were nearly always "un-understanding" of people. And perhaps unreasonably I felt that they were on the lookout for people running after them.

I wrote to Mr. Lewis and asked him if I could talk to him. Immediately I received a note from him at Magdalen College, suggesting that I come to see him. I went to his room, and I could not believe that this now famous man, was sitting with an old slipper dangling from his foot, and that his pullover was a little holey. He had a kind, rosy face, and reminded me so much of the nice, homely farmers of my home surroundings. Many townspeople have no idea of the fine, superior breeding and intellects of the best types of farmers.

Mr. Lewis and I were soon chatting and I told him how unhappy I was; and how desperately anxious I was about my children. I mentioned that it was because of *The Screwtape Letters* that I thought he would understand that I was genuine, and needed kindness. He then told me how funny it was that he had tried over and over again to write something that he could get across; and then quite suddenly he had awakened one morning to find himself famous. He said that if I had an urge to write, I must go on and on, and in fact I would find I had to. I asked him how he knew so much about human beings, as to be able to write *The Screwtape Letters*. He smiled and said, "I only had to know myself really well."

From then on life became easier at Oxford. I visited Mr. Lewis occasionally and just before one of these occasions, I had another blow. We were trying to get a tribunal's permission to allow us to repossess our farm, as my son wanted to farm it. At the hearing my solicitor questioned a rogue of a cowman we had employed in the past, who had spread rumors about the farm stock at the sale after my husband's death, and had then bought the best cows at knock-down prices. I did not know the solicitor was going to do it, but was horrified to find later that the cowman was claiming that an agricultural tribunal was not privileged like a court of law, and he intended to sue me, not the solicitor, for damages for libel.

I wrote in some distress to Mr. Lewis, for advice, and I suppose, comfort. He wrote back saying that he had established a fund to help people in trouble, and he would contribute towards the cost of a defense. The chairman of the tribunal took up the matter, however, and the cowman dropped the case. This incident let me know that Mr. Lewis had established a fund to help people.

When Mr. Lewis died I was terribly sorry that I had stopped writing to him, just when, perhaps, he could have been cheered by letters from friends. As stated, I only stopped writing in case he felt embarrassed because of one foolish woman's accusations. I have wished I could tell him why I did not write. Mr. Lewis was a good friend, and is one of my happy memories. I should like him to know that I qualified as a social worker and became the boarding-out officer for my county. My daughter became well enough to marry. My son has a very good job, and is married with two children. I suppose Mr. Lewis knows this. And I hope he knows how much he helped me when I was almost desperate.

(Mrs.) Joan B. Pile
England, 1969

Part D: With Women at College

Muriel Jones

> *In what is generally considered to be one of Lewis's finest books,* A Preface to Paradise Lost,[1] *at the beginning of chapter fourteen he remarks how much his understanding has been helped by Miss Muriel Bentley. He quoted her, and develops the whole chapter on her remarks. Again, he quotes her in a letter,[2] stressing the excellence of her Miltonic interpretation. I thought she might be a don or a fellow or an authority on Milton. She was nothing of the sort. She was a student, aged twenty-one, of Somerville College. She is now Mrs. E.W. Jones. Her husband is vicar of a parish near Coventry. I went up to see her, and there we were, incredible as it seems, having tea in a vicarage overlooking a meadow with grazing horses and, far off, the slender spire of Coventry Cathedral on the skyline. I told her how Lewis's politesse had led me to believe she was another authority on* Paradise Lost. *That, I said, is the impression he gives, isn't it?*

Yes. It's ridiculous. All he had from me were examination papers. It was generally thought in the university that he didn't care much for women. My tutor tried to induce Mr. Lewis to take me and another girl as pupils and he refused. He just didn't want us. He said he was very busy with the Home Guard, and he always got flu in the Hilary term. My tutor was amused when she told us of these obvious excuses. Oxford was then a very masculine place. You had the feeling that women were there rather on sufferance. Women were not allowed to be members of the (Debating) Union. They weren't allowed in Pusey House or in the chapel at Pusey House. The sermons in Pusey Chapel were quite famous. Different people gave the sermons. I daresay Lewis gave one or two. But women weren't allowed to attend. I think Lewis belonged to that Oxford tradition that saw Oxford in this old-fashioned, Victorian, masculine way. I think he did.

If Lewis had married in his twenties he wouldn't have been the great teacher he was. If he'd been raising a family he would have had far less time. I think it was a good thing he didn't. He was an extremely good teacher. He made you want to read whatever books he mentioned. He taught that the text of anything you are reading is to be taken seriously. You have to try to understand it as the author meant it, not as you fancy it. That has stayed with me very firmly.

I remember his sermon, "Learning in Wartime."[3] He said people have always lived on the edge of a precipice; even times we think were quiet, such as the Victorian Era, were really full of crises. I reread that sermon the other day because you were coming. I remember his saying that you always think things are going to be remarkable, but on the whole, day-to-day life never is, even in wartime. If you are an Army officer you find yourself counting pots of jam. If you are a clergyman you find yourself organizing a choir outing, and such like. If you are allowed to attend Oxford and study, you should get on with it, even in wartime. A life of learning, humbly offered, is a good thing. I took that in too. And it has permanently modified my attitude to things. I don't grumble if life consists of lots of pots of jam, and so on. I can still hear him saying that very clearly.

> *Mrs. Jones's remark on Satan's followers—which she kindly allows me to quote—so impressed Lewis that he used it twice himself. "Mammon," she wrote, "proposes an ordered state of sin with such majesty of pride that we are almost led astray. Perhaps Milton has touched here so essentially the nature of sin that if it were not for the suspicious live to ourselves [II, 254] we should not recognize it as such, so natural is it to man."*

— 8 —

Reactions From Other Women

Kathryn Lindskoog

Mrs. Lindskoog of California is the author of three books about Lewis. She visited him in Oxford. When she had sent him a copy of her master's thesis on the Narnian Chronicles, he had replied in a letter that she was "dead on target," that she "understands my work better than anyone I know, even better than I do myself" (Cambridge, October 29, 1957).[1] She was guest speaker at the C.S. Lewis Institute IV at Seattle Pacific University, 1981. She lectures occasionally.

Was C.S. Lewis a woman hater? Owen Barfield, his friend and solicitor, said that Lewis could properly be called a misogynist on the theoretical level. As a feminist and a Lewis lover, I wish I could disprove that claim.

Fortunately, Mr. Barfield went on to assure people that Lewis was not at all a misogynist in his personal life. I can bear witness to that, and I will. When Glen GoodKnight invited me to speak (at Mythcon V), he suggested that I tell about my own encounter with Lewis. I'll do that and more. I'll tell you about Lewis and eight women who encountered him—Flora, Hope, Janie, Joy, Kathryn, Caroline, Kathleen, and Kaye. These include his mother, his cousin, his foster mother, his wife, a student, a church executive, a poet and an editor.

The first woman in his life was, I think, the most important. This was Florence Augusta Hamilton Lewis of Belfast. She was the daughter of an eloquent Irish preacher who sometimes wept in the pulpit and his

77

bright and eccentric wife, Mary, who excelled in logic but ran a very topsy-turvy—and dirty—home. From this peculiar background the second daughter, Florence Augusta, called Flora, was sent to college to study math. She was brilliant in mathematics and logic and had a calm, sunny disposition.

When Flora was twenty-four, her neighbor Albert Lewis, a young lawyer, told her he was in love with her. Staying calm, sunny, and logical, Flora did not rush into marriage. She kept Albert waiting for eight years and finally married him when she was thirty-two years old. She gave birth to their first son, Warren Hamilton Lewis, when she was thirty-three. She named him after her parents. When she was thirty-six, she gave birth to her second and last child and named him Clive Staples Lewis. Why she named her baby "Clive Staples" is a mystery. Since the Lewis family history consists of eleven volumes, each containing some 300 pages of single-spaced typing, I hope we will eventually learn what Flora had in mind. All we know is that when he was four she gave in to the sensible and stubborn decision that he be called Jack from then on. This nickname was chosen by Lewis himself.

Flora Lewis was a tutor and companion to her boys, and then when Jack was only nine and she was forty-six, she died of cancer. She died on her husband's forty-fifth birthday, when the quotation on his calendar was Shakespeare's line: "Men must endure their going hence" ("King Lear," V,ii). Her husband always kept that page on his calendar, and that line is now inscribed on the tombstone shared by the two Lewis brothers.

Flora's death was the end of the old world for Albert Lewis and his two sons. Their home was never happy again. One can only speculate about how Flora's personality and early death shaped C.S. Lewis's later life.

There is one glaring contrast between C.S. Lewis and his mother. She was gifted in math and he was a dunderhead in math. Even with special remedial tutoring he could not pass the entrance test in math to enable him to attend Oxford, and he was fortunate to be admitted by a waiver for World War I veterans. His grasp of mathematical concepts was fine, but he disliked ordinary computation. It has been claimed that Lewis could not even understand the difference between net and gross and had to be restrained by Owen Barfield from giving away more money than he cleared. His generosity was great. But I do not believe his ignorance was great. He knew net from gross.

It has been said that Jack's brother, Warren Lewis, was so inept at figures that he got the unreasonable idea that he was poor in his last years and took to smoking a certain cheap brand of cigarettes which he disliked just in order to get the coupons that came with them in order to cash them in for free socks. It is a fact that there was some delightful eccentricity in the family along with the brilliance. Both qualities came from both sides of the family.

Unfortunately, no words from Flora Lewis about her son Jack or anything else are yet available in print. However, we can pause briefly to hear the words of Flora's lovely Belfast cousin, Hope (Charlotte Hope Ewart Harding). Hope was no doubt one of the first women who ever met Jack, and she knew him well. When he was fourteen, she called him Jacko and wrote to his father, "I always knew he was a remarkable boy, besides being one of the more lovable I ever came across." (If you have read his autobiography, you know that he did not describe himself so kindly at that awkward age.)

Five years after Cousin Hope called Jack one of the most lovable boys she ever came across, another woman wrote in a letter, "Jack has been so good to me. My poor son asked him to look after me if he did not come back. He possesses, for a boy of his age, such a wonderful power of understanding and sympathy." Those are the words of Mrs. Janie King Askins Moore. Lewis was nineteen and Mrs. Moore was forty-six. If she thought he had already been good to her then, she should have foreseen the thirty-three years to come. Lewis stuck with her until she died.

The story of this involvement is familiar to people who know Lewis's life. Paddy Moore had taken Jack home to meet his middle-aged mother and younger sister, Maureen, before the two boys were shipped to France. Albert Lewis failed to heed Jack's urgent pleading to come and see him for perhaps the last time when he was leaving for the front, and he refused to come to England to see him afterwards when he was recuperating from wounds in the hospital. Mrs. Moore was there both times to fill the gap. Mrs. Moore was reportedly still attractive at forty-six. That was the very age Flora had been when Jack lost her. In his loneliness, Jack became temporarily infatuated with Mrs. Moore. They started living together as mother and son. He tended to call her "Minto," the name of a candy she liked.

Aside from being forty-six years old, Mrs. Moore had little in common with the long-lost Flora. Mrs. Moore had the opposite of a sunny disposition and was never calm or logical. She never bothered to read a book, and she talked mainly about herself. As time went on, Jack became a Christian and she became an atheist. When he was at home she interrupted him ruthlessly to help her with household work or errands. She also had her teen-aged daughter, Maureen, and a couple of maids and a gardener, of course, but the house was always in a tumult and every day seemed to bring new crises. If you listen to Lewis's tapes on love you will find Mrs. Moore's quarrels with her daughter briefly described midway through *storge,* although of course she is not identified by name. In her last years, Mrs. Moore became bedfast and ended up in a nursing home where Lewis visited her every day. She finally died in 1951.

Perhaps Paddy Moore was better off being killed in the war than he would have been if he had lived all those years with his mother, who claimed shortly after his death, "I just lived my life for my son . . . ." At least C.S. Lewis, her unofficial foster son, was spared the burden of having her live her life just for him. Her daughter, Maureen, was the one who had to endure that burden after Paddy had gone. Maureen, now Lady Dunbar of Hempriggs, has so far remained silent about her years in the C.S. Lewis household.

It was 1951, the year Mrs. Moore died, when a book was published in America entitled *These Found the Way.* It includes an essay by the writer, Helen Joy Davidman Gresham, telling how she had moved from atheism to Christianity. The very next year Joy made another move— from America to England—and arrived with her two sons on C.S. Lewis's doorstep. What she had not mentioned in her essay was that the books by Lewis had influenced her conversion and that she, like many other Lewis readers, had been exchanging letters with him. She and Jack became good friends until he realized her romantic intentions and started hiding when he saw her coming up his walk. She returned to America for a divorce from her husband, who was involved with another woman, and returned to England to resume her friendship with Jack.

Five years after Mrs. Moore died, in 1956, the British government refused to renew Joy's permit to remain in England; no one seems to know why. On April 23, Jack actually married her in secret, in a civil ceremony, to enable her to stay in England permanently—but not to enable her to move in with him. He was still a bachelor. He made this very clear in a legal document that he drew up at the time. His feelings for Joy had moved from *agapē* (Christian love) to *philia* (friendship). He had no idea they were to keep on moving.

It was three days before Jack's civil marriage to Joy that I wrote to him for the first time to ask if I could hear him lecture or meet him while I was studying at the University of London that summer. I wrote to him from my college town in Redlands, California. I realize now that my address probably reminded him of Redlands, England, where Mrs. Moore had lived when he got involved with her. I carelessly signed my letter to him "Sincerely, Kay Stillwell," without indicating my sex or marital status.

Mails went faster in those days, and on the day after his civil marriage to Joy he wrote to me the following letter:[2]

> Dear Mr. (or Miss? or Mrs.?) Stillwell:
>
> How nice to hear from anyone who still believes in adjectives and calls them the "Narnian," not the "Narnia" series.
>
> For most of July I shall be at the Kilns, Headington Quarry, Oxford, and happy to arrange a meeting if you are there.
>
> Yours sincerely,
> C.S. Lewis

I stopped at Wheaton College for a conference on the way east in June and met Dr. Clyde Kilby there. He said he was surprised that Lewis would agree to see me, since he was said to be a woman hater. The previous year, Dr. Kilby had gone to meet Lewis and had left Mrs. Kilby out in the car for fear that her female presence would offend Lewis.

As soon as I arrived in London I wrote to Lewis again. This time he answered:[3]

> Dear Miss Stillwell,
>   Friday the 20th is the only day that is possible. Will you meet me for tea at the Royal Oxford Hotel (just outside the railway station) at 4 o'clock? I do not ask you to this house because you would never be able to find it, and, even if you did, it is so far out that most of your time would be taken up en route.
>
> Yours sincerely,
C.S. Lewis

I took the train to Oxford, left my little bag at a cheap hotel room, and set off for the Royal Oxford. As I approached it I became panicky. I did not even know what the man looked like! I entered the hotel in a state of intense fear and hope, and there in the lobby, Lewis arose from the sofa where he was awaiting me and had me sit down next to him. The fact that I was sitting on the same sofa with him made me afraid that I would fall off the sofa. I was giddy with awe.

I had discovered Lewis two years before this meeting, and he had dominated my intellectual life from that time on. The time, place, and manner of my discovering Lewis is of passing interest, at least to me. Flora Lewis's death took place on August 23, 1908, when she was forty-six years old. It was forty-six years after Flora's death, on August 23, 1954, when one of my boyfriends brought me a Lewis book from the public library to see how I would like it. You could say that I was mentally "married" to Lewis that very day. A few years later I married the boyfriend who had brought me the book. My commitments to Lewis and to my husband both took place in Santa Ana, which is the Spanish way of saying St. Anne's. (St. Anne's, where the Pendragon and his company lived, is a place name in *That Hideous Strength*.)

So I had come all the way from Santa Ana to Oxford, and the first thing Lewis did was to pull out his cigarettes and offer me one. I had to confess I did not smoke, and like another man I know who met him later, for once I wished I did. But Lewis congratulated me and advised me never to get started, and I felt better. He said he wished he had never started.

I told him that I was glad that he would see me, because he was said to be a woman hater who avoided women altogether. He took that as a big joke and enjoyed it. He asked me if people did not realize that he had always had female students. Then he told me that there was one woman he certainly would avoid—a crazy woman (I think he said American, but I am not sure), who wrote him letters all the time proposing marriage. He said he would not even open her envelopes any more. He never mentioned the fact that he had lived about thirty-three years with Mrs. Moore and much of that time with her daughter, and that he was now already legally married to his American friend, Joy Davidman.

The tea that Lewis ordered was served on a large, low table before us—a platter full of breads and cookies and a big pot of tea and pitcher of milk, with cups and saucers and spoons. I knew the British had a certain way of pouring tea and milk simultaneously. But I was so new there I did not know how it was done. Lewis did not give me an opening to admit that I would prefer to have him to it; he just asked me to serve and went on talking to me. I lifted the tea and held it aloft for a very long time while we talked on about various subjects. The pot got heavier and heavier. To save myself, I cannot remember how I eventually poured it or how it should have been poured. But I clearly remember that on page eleven of *Out of the Silent Planet,* Lewis wrote: "Ransom, who was very thirsty indeed by now, observed that his host was one of those irritating people who forget to use their hands when they begin talking." At the time he did not show a flicker of irritation.

Lewis was extremely easy to talk with. We soon learned that we had something in common—a love for the surf. When he told me how much he enjoyed the surf in Ireland, I knew he would love it in Southern California. But he told me he had no desire ever to come to the United States.

He did not mention to me that he had done his share of skinny-dipping in his day, and I would not have guessed it. By the time I met him he was fifty-seven years old, bulky and balding with a large, ruddy face, and did not look like a swimmer at all. But he certainly looked full of fun.

I told him that I had read Chad Walsh's book about him and that I had encountered Chad Walsh about three weeks earlier at Wheaton College. He replied that he thought Walsh's book was poor. For example, Walsh accidentally stated that Lewis lived in a rambling, forty-room home. Lewis laughed and told me that the Kilns was a small, modest house. He must have liked Chad Walsh more than he indicated to me, because four years later he dedicated *The Four Loves* to Walsh.

Lewis's latest book when I met him was *Till We Have Faces*. He told me that the publisher had refused to use his own choice for the title. He was still irritated about that. The title he had wanted to use was *Bareface*. He had finally suggested *Till We Have Faces* as a second choice, but he still thought *Bareface* was better. (At this time Lewis was hoping for a good reception for this novel which he considered his finest imaginative work. Its poor reception in England shortly after our meeting was to be one of the biggest disappointments of his career.)

The book, of course, is the one he dedicated to Joy Davidman, a fact which he did not mention to me. He had written it during their friendship. I have heard it said that this is the only novel in which a male author has used an ugly woman for his heroine. It is inevitable that some Lewis readers look for and find connections between the heroine and Joy Davidman.

Lewis told me that *Till We Have Faces* would be his last book with his present publisher. He said it would be a difficult break to make, but he was determined to make it. His present publisher had been giving him a hard time for years, he said, referring to a difficult old man there who took advantage of his good nature. He made the martyrdom story dramatic and funny. By checking a Lewis bibliography you can quickly see that after our talk Lewis went right on letting the same company, Geoffrey Bles, publish most of his books for the rest of his life after all. (Bles has now been taken over by Collins.)

Lewis complained to me that *The Screwtape Letters* was greatly overrated. He said he did not see why it should be so popular. He also told me he was a terrible speller and had been all his life. Then he went on to discuss science fiction.

I remember that he recommended Arthur C. Clarke. I asked him if he had ever read anything by Ray Bradbury and he said no. A couple of years later I heard Bradbury speak and got to ask him afterward how he liked C.S. Lewis's space trilogy, and he said he had never heard of it. Now, however, I had read in the Lewis biography a line that indicates that in 1956 he had in fact sampled Bradbury. I conclude that it does not always pay to ask questions.

In fact, I know it does not, because I had a burning question to ask Lewis. "How," I asked, "do you intend for your readers to pronounce the name Aslan?" All he would say was that he did not care, and that I should pronounce it however it seemed best to me. He would not say it.

The one piece of advice that Lewis gave me besides urging me not to smoke was to read for pleasure. Now that I stop to think about it, I have obeyed him on both counts. It was probably when he waxed warm on the topic of pleasure reading that, after a pithy statement or illustration of his, I exclaimed that that was just what he had written in such and such a book.

He pretended to be crestfallen and said, "That's the trouble with writing a book. Once people have read it, your conversation is not new to them!"

By the time we got up and left the Royal Oxford, Lewis had spent an hour and a quarter with me. The peculiar part is that he seemed to enjoy every minute of it. I had a Brownie camera with me and wanted to take his picture but was afraid that he might be offended if I asked, so I did not. He shook my hand and headed for his bus. I walked down the street in a daze, looking at the hand that he had touched. That night I wrote to my friend John Lindskoog, "C.S. Lewis is the kindest man I have ever met—and his eyes twinkle." You really cannot imagine how they twinkled.

Eight months after my wonderful tea with Lewis, Joy was dying of cancer in the hospital and wanted to go home with Lewis to die as his wife. And so he married her in a Christian ceremony at her bedside. They could not get married in a church, but at least they were married in a place called Churchill Hospital. Jack took her home with him to die, and instead she began to get well!

During World War II some little girls had moved into the Kilns for a time after being evacuated from London, and Lewis had despaired of them because they seemed unable to entertain themselves. He had no such problem when Joy moved in. As soon as she was well enough she delighted in running the household as Jack's bride.

Joy was forty-two when Jack married her, and her sons were about the ages of the two Lewis boys when Flora died. After fifty years, Jack was finally living in a happy family again. His brother, Warren, was there to share in his pleasure. "See how I have dwindled into a husband," Jack liked to remark. The next two years were the happiest time of Lewis's life.

Not everyone liked the new Mrs. Lewis. J.R.R. Tolkien reportedly said years later that it was characteristic of Lewis to be "taken in" by people—notably by Mrs. Moore and Joy Davidman. Tolkien named a third person who had "taken in" Lewis: no less than Charles Williams!

Tolkien's negative attitude toward Mrs. Lewis and Charles Williams reminds readers of his negative attitude toward *The Lion, the Witch and the Wardrobe.* He said to Roger Lancelyn Green, "I hear you've been reading Jack's children's story. It really won't do, you know! I mean to say, 'Nymphs and their Ways, The Love-Life of a Faun.' Doesn't he know what he's talking about?" Tolkien might not have lived long enough to hear about the London *Times* poll in which British children voted for their favorite books, and *The Lion, the Witch and the Wardrobe* came second only to *Charlie and the Chocolate Factory.*

At any rate, Tolkien and some other people did not care for Joy Lewis; but we have Lewis's entire book, *A Grief Observed,* to tell us how he finally felt about his wife. Unfortunately, the only words we have from Joy to tell us about Lewis as a husband were spoken on her deathbed. She said to him, "You have made me very happy." She died of cancer at forty-five, almost the same age Flora had been when she died of cancer fifty-two years earlier.

While Lewis and Joy were enjoying their brief happiness in 1958, another American woman came into his life—Mrs. Caroline Rakestraw of the Episcopal Radio-TV Foundation of Atlanta, Georgia. She arrived in London to supervise the recording of his lectures on "The Four Loves" for American radio. Her comment on his recording session was, "His personality filled the room."

According to Carolyn Keefe's book,[4] Mrs. Rakestraw took it upon herself to snip out and discard parts of the tape about *eros* because she considered it shocking. According to the C.S. Lewis biography, some American bishops considered the *eros* material objectionable even after Mrs. Rakestraw's editing, and made sure that it was not widely broadcast in the United States. Now that there is such a demand for

Lewis material here, they are selling the set of lectures on four cassette tapes.

For one reason or another, Lewis always called Mrs. Rakestraw "Mrs. Cartwheel." Lewis claimed to Walter Hooper that Mrs. Rakestraw said to him, "Professor Lewis, I'm afraid you brought sex into your talks on *eros,*" and Lewis replied, "My dear Mrs. Cartwheel, how can you talk about *eros* and *leave it out?"*

Anyway, Lewis made a book out of his lectures on love and published it in 1960, the year Joy died. The Green and Hooper biography claims that he lost his creativity when she died. That is a pleasantly tragic idea, but I cannot see how the facts support it. Although he was in extremely poor health himself, he finished three more excellent books before he died in 1963.

Incidentally, Corbin Scott Carnell makes a similar claim in his attractive book about Lewis, *Bright Shadow of Reality.* He says that after Charles Williams died in 1945 there was a gap in Lewis's productivity for more than ten years—from 1945 to the late 1950s! Take a look at the list of Lewis's books that came out during that supposed gap. In my own opinion the only death that cut off Lewis's creativity was his own, and I cannot be at all sure of that!

In Lewis's last years he became friends with the poet Kathleen Raine, who was doing research on William Blake at Cambridge. She met Lewis at a dinner party and did not expect to like him very much because she had read only *The Problem of Pain* and *The Screwtape Letters* and did not care for them. But her reaction was, "To meet him was to know that here was a man of great learning continuously kindled into life by imagination. He seemed to possess a kind of boyish greatness." She had tea with him in his rooms at Cambridge occasionally before he had to retire, and she says, "Every conversation was an exploration or a game with a shining ball flying through the air." She became a devoted lover of the Narnian Chronicles.

The very last woman to meet Lewis was Kaye Webb, the editor of Puffin Books. She went to the Kilns two days before he died to make plans about their paperback edition of the Narnian Chronicles. Kaye Webb's reaction to Lewis was, "What a great and dear man. How I wish

I'd had a chance to know him well . . . ."

Shortly before Kaye Webb met him, Lewis said that he hoped that in heaven he would find that Spenser had written another six books of *The Faerie Queene* for him to read there and that Rider Haggard had written a trilogy of romances about the Wandering Jew. Along that line, some of us might wish that in heaven we will find seven more *Chronicles of Narnia* or perhaps the strange romance about Helen of Troy which Lewis could not finish because of failing health.

But a woman in Canada had a more ambitious idea about heaven than reading Lewis books there. Her friend, Dr. Overton Stephens, author of *Today Is All You Have,* was dying of cancer when she left for the summer some years ago. When she came home and found to her surprise that he was still alive, she said joyfully, "Oh, I'm so glad! I want you to make an appointment for me to see Lewis in heaven." Dr. Stephens laughingly agreed to do what he could about it, and he was very soon on his way. I say, "good luck" to that woman.

I have told you a bit about a few of the many women who personally encountered Lewis. From my own experience, I believe that being with Lewis was even better than reading his books. Being with him was a bit of heaven, and I hope that heaven will include a bit of being with him.

— 9 —

A Guest in the House

George Sayer

Professor Sayer was for many years head of the English department at Malvern College, Worcestershire. He was a pupil of Lewis's for three years and a friend for twenty-six years. He is now engaged in writing a new critical biography of Lewis. It is noteworthy that Professor Thomas Howard remarks that: "It is a peculiar trait in us all that makes us want to know everything about a great man. If we can find out how Johnson wanted his eggs, or whether Bismarck wanted the windows open or closed, we will. Data like this may not throw light on the man's contribution to the race (literature, politics, science, etc.), but it often seems to." In this chapter, Professor Sayer sheds light on some of Lewis's habits, preferences, and mannerisms.

Friends who find out that C.S. Lewis often stayed with me frequently ask questions about when he got up, what he ate, and so on. The first thing to understand is that he never wore a watch. I don't really know why this was so. He said once that he could never remember to wind them. On another occasion he said that watches didn't seem to go for him. But I'm inclined to think that not wearing a watch went with his determination to spend as little as possible on himself.[1] Anyway, the result was that he had no idea when to get up in the morning. If one said to him that breakfast would be at eight, he would ask to be called half an hour beforehand. One might find him asleep, surprised that it was morning, or more likely fully dressed and, I suspect, meditating or saying his prayers.

When he first came to stay he appreciated an early morning cup of tea, but in his later years he declined this. I suspect that he still enjoyed it, but regarded it as something that could be given up. He never ceased trying to simplify his life.

Although there is running hot and cold water in my house, I think he always washed with cold water. For shaving, he lathered his face with a stick of shaving soap (I think Erasmic was the brand) and used an ancient brush with an old-fashioned Gillette razor. I think that he usually used cold water for shaving too.

He wore white cotton underwear, I think Aertex, and a white cotton shirt which he usually wore open-necked when he stayed with us, with the wings of the shirt collar outside his old tweed jacket. His trousers were old and baggy and usually made of gray flannel or corduroy.

He used a chamber pot during the night, and emptied it unobtrusively before breakfast, waiting until he was sure that the route to the toilet was clear.

Sometimes he would be down early for breakfast. He might then sit down and read a book, but if the day was fine, he would usually stroll about in the garden or along the road outside the house. He felt especially clear-headed in the morning and, I think, quite often prayed then.

We gave him coffee for his earlier visits, but later on tea, which he preferred. He liked very strong Indian tea, served in large cups with milk. We never offered him eggs and bacon. In his earlier visits, he sometimes had a boiled egg; later on, just toast, butter and marmalade; later on still, bread, butter and marmalade—for he said at that time that he preferred bread to toast. When, later still, he was on a diet, he asked for Ryvita or Vitawheat. Bread in our house was usually whole meal and often made by my wife, but I think that he preferred ordinary white bakers' bread.

He never read a newspaper at breakfast or at any other time. Nor did he ever willingly listen to the radio. If he had a companion he would talk at breakfast as brilliantly as at any other time of day. If he breakfasted alone he would read a book.

After breakfast he made his bed and tidied his bedroom. He was then ready and eager for a walk or for whatever was to be done that day. If there was a delay, perhaps because food had to be prepared and sandwiches made, he would sit down and read.

A favorite midday meal when walking consisted of sandwiches eaten with a pint or two or draught bitter ale. He seemed to like all sorts of sandwiches, meat, cheese, and eggs about equally. His taste in beer was for bitter, but he did not dislike mild as much as his brother, who maintained that it made him sick. He rather disliked all bottled beer and refused it when canned.

His taste in pubs (taverns) where he usually ate his sandwiches, was for the old-fashioned. Provided the place was reasonably clean, he did not mind if it was primitive and uncomfortable. In chilly weather, he enjoyed an open wood or coal fire. He often chatted with the landlord and after the meal, as well as at other times in the day, he would certainly smoke. He chose plain, untipped, non-filter cigarettes, such as Players' Navy Cut.

At about half-past four or five he would long for a cup or two of tea. He did not as a rule eat anything with it. If he did it would be a slice or two of thin bread and butter.

He liked to be home at about 6:00 PM. He would then wash himself pretty well all over, read a passage from any translation of the Bible, and say his prayers. He thought that if he left them until much later in the day, he would be too tired to say them properly.

At about seven he liked to sip a glass or two of dry sherry and to talk. He liked a substantial evening meal and to drink wine with it, though, if wine was not available, beer would do. His taste in food was Irish. He liked plain, roast meat, served with roasted or new potatoes and natural, made-in-the-pan gravy. He did not like vegetables very much, and natural salads hardly at all. He took little interest in fruit or puddings but enjoyed English cheese, especially cheddar or Stilton. He ate all his food extremely fast. He would clear his plate before my wife or I had had much more than three or four forks full. When he had finished a course, he would sit back and talk. He had no liking for elaborate dishes or for continental methods of cooking.

He preferred red wine to white. Again his taste was robust—he thought burgundy a far finer wine than claret, which he once described

91

as thin and acid. He might take two or three glasses of it. Hock was his favorite white wine.

At the end of a meal, he much enjoyed vintage port if any was available. Even more than port he liked brown sherry, a rather unusual taste. He also enjoyed the kind of madeira called Malmsey. He did not like brandy and never smoked a cigar in my house.

He would drink coffee, but after a meal he liked better a cup of tea. He would then sit, read and talk until it was time to go to bed. If he was with suitable friends, he might combine with them to read a great poem aloud.

At about ten he liked to have another cup of tea, and in his younger days some whiskey—for most of his life VAT 69 was the brand he liked best.

He went to bed for choice at about half-past ten or eleven. I think he undressed quickly and was very soon asleep. He disliked a heated bedroom and usually slept with a partly open and uncurtained window. He always declined my wife's offer of a hot-water bottle.

— 10 —

South African View

Peter Philip

Mr. Philip of Cape Town, South Africa, was a pre-war pupil of Lewis's. He is now South African consul-general in Wellington, New Zealand.[1]

When my father offered me the opportunity to become an undergraduate at Oxford, I chose Magdalen College for the following reasons: the dean of divinity at Magdalen, the Rev. Adam Fox, had been a master at my school in Cape Town; because of all the Oxford colleges I had seen, Magdalen was the most beautiful in its setting and architecture; and because C.S. Lewis was its English tutor.

To be honest, the prospect of having Lewis as tutor was the third attraction, not the first. In 1935 his reputation outside the University was only beginning to burgeon and had not penetrated Cape Town. Within the University he was a figure of distinction. To be tutored by him was something to inspire awe and envy. Even ignoramuses had heard of him. The awe and envy have persisted down the years to an ever-increasing degree. Indeed, in appropriate circles, the most effective conversation-stopping gambit I know is—"C.S. Lewis was my tutor at Oxford."

When I went up to Oxford I had certain fixed ideas about how a don should look—elderly, thin, pale, austere, scholarly and rather aloof. Lewis, therefore, came as a shock. He was well-built and almost corpulent. He wore tweed jackets and a deerstalker cap. He smoked a pipe. He drank beer, for the most part. He looked like a well-to-do tenant farmer.

His manner was jovial when he was in a good humor, which I must say was most of the time. I was told that he frequently reduced his female pupils to tears, which I found puzzling. Heaven knows, I was an extremely callow nineteen-year-old, only semi-literate; and I must have been a great trial to him. But he never allowed it to show. On one occasion, I used the word "efficacy" in an essay. Unfortunately I did not know how to pronounce it, and my guess proved to be woefully off course. Lewis looked at me and said, "How interesting that that should be the South African pronunciation. In England we pronounce it 'effikasy' "—which I thought was an extremely kind and tactful method of putting me right.

I cannot say that I ever got close to him or that I ever felt relaxed in his company. I was too immature to meet him on his own ground, and he was too cultivated to be able to come down to mine. I often wish I had met him when I was much older. To have known him when I was a youthful undergraduate was a terrible waste.

His knowledge of English literature was immense and he had a remarkable memory to go with it. I occasionally tried this out by deliberately misquoting from obscure English poets but he always picked up the mistake.

He was most conscientious. In four years I do not remember him missing a weekly tutorial with me more than two or three times. Being a hard worker himself, and a fast and voracious reader, he expected his pupils to be the same, and he found it difficult to condone standards or work or performance which were below his own.

He appeared to have no interest whatever in the sporting activities of the College. Once I tried to persuade him to let me off the weekly essay and tutorials on the grounds that I was required to cox the College eight. This was the only time I saw him really angry. The weekly reading list which he gave me was always well beyond my scope. There were just not enough hours in seven days to absorb that number of books—or at all events, not by me.

Once a week during the term Lewis gave me a tutorial which lasted for one hour, when I read him an essay which I had prepared on a prescribed subject. More often than not I had not slept for twenty-four hours, having sat up all night writing the essay. I always planned to spread my literary researches more evenly through the seven days of the

94

week but I never managed to achieve that worthwhile objective. We would begin with some casual conversation while Lewis lounged on the sofa filling his pipe, and I sat opposite him in an armchair with my literary masterpiece at the ready. This stage did not last long. Lewis had too active a mind to waste time with trivialities. During the reading of the essay, which as a rule took about twenty minutes, Lewis would listen in silence making a note from time to time. Then the inquest would begin.

He never disagreed openly with any opinion which I expressed, however inane it might have been. He would simply require me to defend it against his penetrating criticism until my desperate defense began to disintegrate. Very often he would then change his ground and point out the arguments which I should have used to support my thesis. This procedure was a most effective encouragement to clear thinking and the marshaling of lucid argument.

Lewis used to hold informal evenings in his rooms for the purpose of reading "Beowulf" and of inducing in us a feeling for the Anglo-Saxon language. There were usually about half a dozen of us, seated around the room and armed with mugs of beer. We would read passages in turn, with Lewis taking his turn and declaiming the lines with gusto and evident enjoyment in his deep and rather throaty voice.

I am not sure that Lewis was at his best with young people. Life at Oxford in my day was a fairly light-hearted affair. Frivolity was fashionable and it was considered rather stuffy to take anything seriously. Lewis was not frivolous. I had the impression that he could become impatient and irritated with young men who frittered away their time and had not the wit to recognize the opportunities that they were missing. I would have liked to have seen him in the company of his contemporaries whose talents and maturity matched his own.

And yet, even though he probably found youthful immaturity rather tedious at times, he could be very understanding and helpful, as I discovered on at least two occasions. Toward the end of my third year, it became fairly evident to me—and apparently to him also—that my education had not yet reached the stage at which I was prepared to face the examiners. He took it upon himself to persuade my father and the College to give me a fourth year before writing my finals. I thought this a kind and considerate gesture.

Then again, when my fourth year came to an end and the first day of the final examinations actually arrived, I awoke covered in spots; awkward to the last, I had chosen that moment to contract German measles. If Lewis thought I was a damned nuisance, he never showed it. He was immensely sympathetic and helpful in arranging for an invigilator at a moment's notice so that I could write my finals alone and in isolation in my digs[2]—where incidentally I was much more comfortable and relaxed than I would ever have been in the Examination Schools.

If I were asked which of Lewis's qualities I found most impressive, I believe I would give first priority to his lucidity. It is hardly surprising that he was able to communicate, as a lecturer and as a writer, with such skill. He was a master craftsman. And it was a great privilege to have seen him exercise his craft.

— 11 —

Stunning Effect

Erik Routley

*The Rev. Dr. Routley, Professor of Church Music at
Westminster Choir College, Princeton, New Jersey, U.S.A.,
since September, 1975, is a minister of the (formerly)
Congregational Church of England and Wales (now part of
the United Reformed Church), and was president of that
Church, 1970-1971. He was lecturer in Church History at
Mansfield College from 1948 to 1959; and has held
pastorates in various places in Britain, including Edinburgh
(1959-1967) and Newcastle-upon-Tyne. He was educated at
Magdalen and Mansfield Colleges, Oxford. Of his twenty-
nine books published to date, most deal with hymnology,
church music or church history. Dr. Routley says his
"interest in hymns would not have commended itself to
Lewis."[1]*

I can't say that I met Lewis personally more than two or three
times. But I am glad to set down a few memories which will remain with
me as long as I live.

Oxford, during the years from 1939 to 1945, was a somber place. I
took my first graduation examinations in June, 1940; and I won't soon
forget the invigilator's remark before the first session: "You will be
advised, if our postal services are still in operation, whether you are
required to attend an oral examination." We thought we might well all
be required to speak German by September (those were pre-Eisenhower

days). As I look back on those student days, the one thing I am profoundly thankful for was that they were the years when C.S. Lewis and Charles Williams[2] were doing their astounding "double act" in Oxford. One can't think of one without the other. (Lewis would have been the first to insist on that.) Lewis regarded his Christian lay ministry as his "war work," and did his best to give it up (except for his writings) as soon as the war ended. But what days those were!

From 1936 to 1940 I was an undergraduate at Magdalen, Lewis's college, and until 1939 I didn't know who he was. (Magdalen was an uncomfortable and fragmented society in those years.) But on the second Sunday of the first term of the war, in October, 1939, I saw that he was billed to preach in the University Church. It was odd enough in those days to have a preacher who wasn't a clergyman of the Church of England, and I thought I would go along. The service was to begin at 8:00 PM, and I suppose I arrived about ten minutes before eight. There was hardly a seat to be had. The one I got was right under the pulpit. I could see the preacher only when he was going up the steps. And I said to myself, "So *that's* Lewis!" The church was dim. Only minimal lighting was allowed. Most of us had to sing the hymns from memory. But Lewis gave us the sermon called "Learning in Wartime," which was, I suppose, his debut as a preacher. "A Syrian ready to perish was my father," from Deuteronomy 26, was his text.

I think the next time he preached was in June, 1941, and the sermon was entitled "The Weight of Glory."[3] This time it was a summer evening. Lighting was no problem. But the place was packed solid long before the service began. The last hymn was "Bright the Vision that Delighted." The sermon took three-quarters of an hour to deliver. Its stunning effect is something one can hardly communicate. Just to read it now is to be captivated by its uncanny combination of sheer beauty and severe doctrine. Here, you feel even when reading, and you felt it ten times more when listening, was a man who had been laid hold of by Christ and enjoyed it.

Lewis had a superbly unaffected delivery: a deep voice which went well with his cheerful and bucolic appearance (all pictures of him that I know are good ones). It was a voice that really did vindicate the saying that the medium is the message. No rhetorical tricks: he read every word. Yet the way he used the words as precision tools, the effortless rhythm of the sentences, the scholarship made friendly, the sternness made beautiful—these things all made it impossible for the listener to notice the passing of time. I call this a "vintage" example of his style—it comes from this very sermon:

> At present we are on the outside of the world, the wrong side of the door. We discern the freshness and purity of morning, but they do not make us fresh and pure. We cannot mingle with the splendours we see. But all the leaves of the New Testament are rustling with the rumour that it will not always be so. Some day, God willing, we shall get *in*.

I would counsel any preacher, or any public speaker, to study every letter of that short passage: to notice how many of its words are of one syllable; and what contrasting effect the two-syllable words have. Who else would have spoken of the leaves of the New Testament "rustling"? That is poetry in the service of the Gospel. Well, imagine what it was like to *hear* that.

But Lewis's main work was not preaching: he would do it when asked, but what he probably did more comfortably was more informal. When the term was on, you never knew where you would find him next. John Wain gives a good picture of the Socratic Club in his autobiographical book, *Sprightly Running:* that was the weekly meeting for good-homored and high-level debate, where students crowded into a room and sat on the floor or under the piano, and Lewis took the chair. Somebody, I remember, who had been drinking deep of positivist philosophy, asked in the course of the discussion, "Well, how can you prove anything? I mean, how can you prove there isn't a blue cow sitting on that piano?"

To this Lewis replied, "Well, in what sense *blue?*"

Sometimes learned men would produce a defense of agnosticism, or an assault on Christianity. That was the signal for Lewis to reply. I heard him deliver, *extempore,* a satisfying devastation of such an attempt by A.L. Rowse, a distinguished man of letters. I recall Lewis saying: "Mr. Rowse reminds me of a friend of mine called Bulver, whose wife has perfected what I call the technique of Bulverism. When Mr. Bulver remarked to his wife that the three angles of a triangle together add up to 180 degrees, Mrs. Bulver replied, 'You say that because you're a man.' " The point was, of course, that attributing an argument to a temperament did not invalidate the argument.

Then there was the hilarious occasion when Lewis and Charles Williams were in a double bill in Magdalen College dining hall—I don't know how many hundreds crammed themselves in—to talk about "free love." (That was when the permissive society was still underground.) With terrifying conviviality they demolished "free love" and expounded the Christian teaching on sex. How solemn and boring it would be nowadays if anybody tried to do it!

Lewis said he owed everything to Charles Williams. In a sense he mediated Charles Williams to ordinary people. Williams was a genius, of course. Him, I think, you absolutely had to hear in the flesh. As a writer he is brilliant but tough. As a speaker he was electrifying—that splutting London accent, those streaks of energy that sparked out of him, that faculty for recreating a whole scene of Shakespeare by dancing from one side of the rostrum and taking each part as it came. Williams talked at about 250 words to the minute, Lewis at about half that speed. Williams was a tenor; Lewis was a bass. Williams was thin and intense; Lewis was comfortable and placid. Williams smoked cigarettes; Lewis smoked a pipe. On Williams's sudden death in 1945 Lewis wrote unforgettably, "When he died it was our idea of death that changed."

My final memory of those otherwise dim Oxford days is sitting up into the small hours, night after night, with the first edition of Lewis's early book, *The Pilgrim's Regress*[4]—the one without the preface and the running headline—working out what it was all about: getting inside this "north-south" pattern, and all the allegorical references on every page. I did this with my friend who shared my lodging and is now my brother-in-law. We took some satisfaction, when the explained edition of the book came out, that we had pretty well got it right. That, I remember, and the *Summa Theologica* of St. Thomas Aquinas, more or less kept us sane.

I know myself what others know far better—how unfailingly courteous Lewis was in answering letters. I think I corresponded with him on three or four occasions. If I said I was on the outer fringe of his acquaintance I would probably be doing myself more than justice. I can't ever have been more to him than just one more confounded writer of letters. But there was a reply every time. It might be quite brief. Lewis had a habit of writing all his letters continuously on a sheet of typing paper and snipping them off in strips.[5] But it was always written for *you,* and nobody else.

I think this was his great secret. He hated casual contacts: human contact must, for him, be serious and concentrated and attentive, or else it was better avoided. It might be for a moment only; but that was its invariable quality.

That is why so many people have precious memories of him, why he could not write three words without the reader feeling they were written for him and for him alone, why his massive books of scholarship read as delightfully as his children's stories, and why he is one of the few preachers who can be read without losing his message.

True courtesy has its roots in precision, not in casualness. That is true of personalities and of writers. If ever there was a man who exploded the slander that "academic" means remote, dull and inhuman, that man was Lewis.

If this is true it explains why he is at present, in his own country, so scandalously undervalued, especially among theologians. His courtesy was formidable. His skill was never unkind. Qualities like that are pretty low on our stock exchange right now. We know that J.B. Phillips said about him in *The Ring of Truth:* how, shortly after Lewis's death, Lewis came into his room and was present with him for a moment, "A *red* vision, glowing with health."[6] Having met both Lewis and Phillips, I entirely believe in the veracity of that vision. My best wish would be that he would from time to time haunt you, just like that.

— 12 —

Memories

H.C. Chang

Mr. Chang was born in China and graduated from the University of Shanghai and earned a PhD for a thesis on Elizabethan drama at Edinburgh University. For some years he was Lecturer in English at the University of Malaya in Singapore; and is now University Lecturer in Chinese Studies, Fellow of Wolfson College, Cambridge, and author of Allegory and Courtesy in Spenser[1], Chinese Literature: Vol. I, Popular Fiction and Drama[2] *and* Chinese Literature: Vol.II, Nature Poetry.[3]

I first met the late C.S. Lewis in June, 1952, in his rooms in Magdalen College, Oxford. As had been arranged, I called at 12:00. He was finishing a tutorial, and I remember distinctly that the reading list he was giving his two pupils ended with Aureng-zebe.[4] I had been working on Spenser at Edinburgh with Professor W.L. Renwick, and had wanted so much to meet Mr. Lewis; I was also anxious to show him the translation of a Chinese allegory that I had done. When, after some preliminary exchanges, he learned that I was at work on the ideal of courtesy in *The Faerie Queene,* he said that he found the courtier ideal a little vulgar in comparison with the ideal of the medieval knight in Malory.[5] And he quoted some lines from Book II of *The Faerie Queene* to illustrate his point. I myself was a lover of medieval chivalry and was disposed to agree with him. Nevertheless, I thought that medieval chivalry also had its limitations, and spent some minutes arguing this.

Somewhat awed by him, I did not then realize, as I have since come to think, though it may seem presumptuous on my part to claim it, that we had much in common. For his hero was Sir Philip Sidney (as I discovered much later in reading Sir Maurice Bowra's autobiography) and Sidney, too, was mine. And indeed Sidney had embodied in his life both chivalry and courtesy. My ingrained belief that a definite code ought to govern the tone of one's writing as well as one's conduct— which in essence is Confucian but uninfluenced by European chivalry— must have appealed to C.S. Lewis and made him readier, in later years, to accept me as a friend. Certainly a vein of chivalry underlies all his own writings, and this explains for me the style and verve of his literary criticism. It is the criticism of someone with a great deal of learning and insight, and a real sense of obligation towards his subject, his readers and himself.

In the course of our first conversation he told me that it had taken him nine years to write *The Allegory of Love* and fifteen to write *English Literature in the Sixteenth Century,* which he had just finished and which was not to appear until 1954. He also said that there was 'nothing new' on Spenser in the latter, meaning, I suppose, that his views had not altered since writing the former. We also discussed the state of the world and China under communism. I remember taking my leave of him at a quarter to one and then getting lost in the cloisters at Magdalen, so that I met him again, a few minutes later, going to his lunch.

He had agreed to read my Chinese allegory and, when I posted the manuscript to him from Edinburgh, went to considerable trouble to comment on it. This was not the only act of kindness which he showed me. As for my indebtedness to him, it also went beyond this. For he was a bright star on my horizon. After reading *The Allegory of Love,* I looked at *The Faerie Queene* and indeed all allegorical literature with different eyes.

In 1954 he moved to Cambridge to become Professor of Medievel and Renaissance English. I had also moved to Cambridge the year before. I attended some of his lectures on Milton and, on November 29, his Inaugural Lecture, 'De Descriptione Temporum,' which was an exhilarating experience. In the lecture he introduced himself as a specimen of 'Old Western Man.' I was, then and since, inclined to emulate his example and regard myself as Old Eastern or Old Chinese Man, but feared that I had already become too westernized to be able to claim this truthfully.

When my book *Allegory and Courtesy in Spenser* was published in 1955, I sent a copy to him, and he invited me shortly afterwards to lunch in Magdalene College. He had only been able to glance at the book but made it clear that he would read it later. He also asked me a question which at the time I quite misunderstood. The gist of it was whether people from different provinces in China, when reading the same poem aloud, would pronounce the words so differently as not to be mutually intelligible. It was not until two and a half years later, when I saw him again, that I picked up the thread of our previous conversation and answered the question. For shortly after that lunch, I left for Singapore.

In May, 1958, I was on leave from Singapore and, late one afternoon, called on him in his rooms in Magdalene College, Cambridge. He gave me to understand that he approved of my book and asked if there had been any 'interesting reactions.' I told him about a review that Dr. Janet Spens had written in the *Review of English Studies*. To show him the kind of teaching I had been doing in Singapore and Kuala Lumpur, I produced an examination paper I had set for my first-year students of English literature, in which he expressed some interest.

When, towards the end of October, 1959, I returned to Cambridge to become a University Lecturer in Chinese, I looked forward to meeting him again. C.S. Lewis had become a friend, though I held him no less in reverence. But my teaching kept me extremely busy and I did not see him as often as I would have liked. In November, 1960, he came to tea at our house on Milton Road and met my wife and my daughter (an admirer of his children's books from the age of nine), Miss Carmen Blacker, Miss Hiro Ishibashi and Mrs. G. Dudbridge, who was then my pupil, were also present. My wife had just recovered from post-natal depression and spoke about her unaccountable weeping during her illness. Lewis then told us how once, after taking an examination, he had suddenly burst into tears. On his way to our house he had walked past the roundabout at Mitcham's Corner. He described it as 'murderous' and advised me to stop cycling. He himself had never been able to learn to drive a car.

In May, 1963, he sent me a post card; he wrote that he had some copies of a Chinese translation of *The Magician's Nephew*[6] which he wanted to give away. I called on him in Magdalene the next morning and had nearly an hour's pleasant chat in the company of an American lady from his U.S. publishers. He was in high spirits and said that he could drink all he liked but not eat, from which I gathered that he had been ill. At the time, beards were coming into fashion, and one of us suggested a connection between beards and existentialism. I received the books from him and left shortly before 1:00.

Though I am not psychic, I had an unusual experience about six months later. Under Sunday, November 24, 1963, the entry in my diary reads: 'A gloomy weekend. Yesterday afternoon I was filled with an oppressive feeling I could not explain; it was a kind of foreboding of disaster, but in the morning I felt better. This noon, the one o'clock BBC news announced the death of CSL.'

— 13 —

Surprise Encounter

Naoyuki Yagyu

Naoyuki Yagyu is Professor of English at Kanto Gakuin University, Yokohama, and chancellor of the Kanto Gakuin System of Schools. He has translated into Japanese three of Lewis's books: Miracles, Mere Christianity, *and* The Great Divorce; *and is now working on one of his own:* C.S. Lewis—His Faith and Literary Achievements.

In 1942 I was a sophomore in the English department of Tokyo University of Literature and Science. Among the many courses offered there was one labeled, "Principles of English Literary History." The professor's aim seemed to be to attain a "perfect" history of English literature by comparing and criticizing traditional books such as Taine's, Saintsbury's, Legouis-Cazamian's, Elton's, and others.

One day the professor discussed the "revaluation" of English literature in the twenties and thirties of the present century. Apparently, he mentioned the names of some "Miltonoclasts" such as T.S. Eliot, Ezra Pound, F.R. Leavis, and others, and must have referred to Leavis's famous book, *Revaluation*. I don't remember well. For most of his highly erudite lectures went over my head. But one thing I clearly remember: he showed us a copy of E.M.W. Tillyard's *Milton*. It must have been the first edition. It was twice as thick as the modern editions. The name of the author stuck in my mind, because at that time I decided to choose *Paradise Lost* as the subject of my graduation thesis.

So I began to read Tillyard's *Milton*. It took me two or three months to finish it. But oh, the sense of fulfillment when I finally closed the book! It was the first academic work I, a student with a poor English vocabulary, had ever read. I thought the book was an adequate answer to anti-Miltonist arguments. In a word, Dr. Tillyard became my sacred cow.

Then a disquieting rumor reached my ears—a rumor that a young scholar at Oxford found fault with Dr. Tillyard and provoked some controversy. Hearing this, I said to myself, "What an insolent chap! Whoever puts up his nose at the great Doctor Tillyard shall be my mortal enemy."

In short, the "mortal enemy" turned out to be C.S. Lewis. That's why I began to read him. The first book I laid my hands on was *The Personal Heresy*, in which the above-mentioned controversy is fully recorded. And the result was this: "Well, Lewis isn't bad at all. To begin with, he is not one of those Miltonoclasts that I have no stomach for. And his style is so captivating. Look at this again:

> The poet is not a man who asks me to look at *him:* he is
> a man who says, 'look at that,' and points; the more I follow
> the pointing of his finger the less I can possibly see of *him.*

It's hard to beat him there. Dr. Tillyard lacks this sort of clincher: he is too calm, too gentle, if not too drab."

Next, I read *A Preface to Paradise Lost*. It didn't take more than two pages of the book to knock me down. In the 'Dedication to Charles Williams,' he writes:

> When the old poets made some virtue their theme they
> were not teaching but adoring, and what we take for the
> didactic is often the enchanted . . . . Apparently, the door of
> the prison was really unlocked all the time; but it was only
> you who thought of trying the handle. Now we can all come
> out.

Limited space prevents me from explaining why and how this made me lie prostrate before C.S. Lewis. All I can say is, "Whoso readeth, let him understand." *A Preface* was followed (in the order of my reading) by

The Allegory of Love. Here, I cannot but quote the enchanting line at the end of chapter one (the author referring to the last stanzas of Troilus and to the 'recantation' by Chaucer and Malory):

> We hear the bell clang; and the children, suddenly hushed and grave, and a little frightened, troop back to their master.

I was mesmerized by this and heaved a long sigh of soul-intoxicating gratification.

Thus, the C.S. Lewis I first came to know was an Oxford scholar of English literature, splendid stylist, and magical metaphor-maker, rather than "a talent for putting old-fashioned truths into a modern idiom." At any rate, I continued to read his academic works: *English Literature in the 16th Century, Studies in Words, An Experiment in Criticism, The Discarded Image, Spenser's Images of Life,* and so on. Here, I must adduce a quotation from *An Experiment:*

> Milton, hanged, drawn and quartered by two or three influential critics—and their disciples all said Amen— seems to have revived.

This, I think, is a most effectively satirical answer to F.R. Leavis's famous oracle: "Milton's dislodgement, in the past decade, after his two centuries of predominance, was effected with remarkably little fuss." For that matter, who could have said this in one of the forbidding O.H.E.L. volumes?

> A man can only say, 'Bless thee, Horace, thou art translated.'

I am not sure when I became acquainted with Lewis' more popular books, for which he is better known. Probably, it was in 1955 or 1956, and the first book I happened to read seems to have been a small booklet called *Broadcast Talks.* I was fascinated by the book and farther driven on to *Christian Behaviour, Beyond Personality, Miracles, The Screwtape Letters, The Great Divorce,* etc. While reading these books, I definitely became a (would-be) disciple of Lewis and came to look upon him as my spiritual mentor.

To me, his magnetism still resides in his style. Don't misunderstand me. 'Style' cannot exist apart from content or meaning. What I mean is that his way of saying things is as delightful as the things themselves. The following passage is an example of this:

> Almost the whole of Christian theology could perhaps be deduced from the two facts: (a) That men make coarse jokes, and (b) That they feel the dead to be uncanny.

> There comes a moment when the children who have been playing at burglars hush suddenly: *was* that a real footstep in the hall? There comes a moment when people who have been dabbling in religion ('Man's search for God'!) suddenly draw back. Supposing we really found Him? We never meant it to come to *that!* Worse still, supposing He had found us?[1]

If regular theologians could ever use such language, I would immediately become an avid reader of modern—otherwise dry-as-dust—theology. The following are the final sentences of *Reflections on the Psalms:*

> "How he's grown!" we exclaim, "How time flies!" as though the universal form of our experience were again and again a novelty. It is as strange as if a fish were repeatedly surprised at the wetness of water. And that would be strange indeed; unless of course the fish were destined to become, one day, a land animal.

By means of this metaphor what is Lewis doing? Well, he is proving, no, not proving, but *has proved* that Heaven and Hell exist. This last quotation, I think, provides us with the epitome of Lewis's whole personality: his faith and imagination, his spiritual insight and literary craftsmanship.

While innocently reading Lewis's books, I was gradually drawn into his magic circle. It is too late to get out. But, readers, rest assured; I found in the depth of my soul how joyful and free it is to be imprisoned there. All I should do now is not try to get out, but rather go "Farther up and farther *in!"*

— 14 —

Poet to Poet

Ruth Pitter

Ruth Pitter is the first woman to have won the Queen's Medal[1] for poetry.[2] "Why didn't someone tell me?" asked Lewis after first reading her work. His letters[3] to Miss Pitter fill a volume about one inch thick. Lewis once confided to his close friend, Hugo Dyson, "I am not a man for marriage; but if I were, I would ask R.P."[4] Miss Pitter lives in a homey old brick house on a quiet road in Long Crendon, Buckinghamshire, about twelve miles from Oxford. I visited her there and taped her remarks.

The first time I saw Lewis was in his rooms. I was introduced by Herbert Palmer, an eccentric poet. Palmer was determined to bring Lewis out as a poet. Lewis was a very good poet-craftsman; more of a word master than an inspired poet. He could do anything with words except, perhaps, the true poetic magic. In his *Allegory of Love*,[5] for example, what he does with the really old stuff! Doing it into modern English and hardly changing it! He was a great word master. But when poetry happens, something magical happens. He never quite attained to that in verse. But he has some wonderful verses.

Well, my visit was arranged. I went to see him and he said, "I can give you half an hour," just as though he was talking to a student. He didn't know me at all. I knew him. I mean I knew he was a great author, though I hadn't read his literary studies. I had only read his *Broadcast Talks*.[6] The first one of these I heard Lewis broadcast was such good entertainment I gathered everybody to listen to the next one. He was saying how sex had gone wrong. He said it was hushed up because it had gone wrong. Lewis said if you could fill a theater by offering a sort of striptease act about food (bring a covered plate on the stage, and just before the lights went out, lift off the cover and expose two mutton chops!), wouldn't you think something had gone wrong with the audience's appetite for food? It made me laugh. I howled with laughter. I wasn't a committed Christian then. If I had only known I was hooked. I became a practicing Christian after that. By tuning in to these talks, which I thought were very amusing, I was hooked before I knew.

Once I heard him lecture in London: and I've never seen such a crowd before. I mean such a variety of people. It was in a big hall with a gallery. There were several old ladies, perhaps retired lady dons, in front rows, checking their hearing aids, you know, and beaming in anticipation. And behind them a good many well-known people, nearly all with people they shouldn't have been with, and glorying in it. I was in the side gallery where I could see nearly everybody. There were plenty of earnest Christians, also beaming, in the body of the hall. Up in the near gallery were more well-known people, not courting the limelight. A few distinguished authors appeared occasionally, taking a quick look over the edge of the gallery and popping back. When Lewis came in he was full of *bonhomie* and smiling at the vast applause; and he began by saying, "This is a very *warm* poem!" Of course the Christians were out to hear Lewis on any subject, the dons for the learned exposition, and the scandalous for the "warmth."

It was a pleasure to hear his splendid voice, never a dull phrase, and hardly any notes, and he looked straight at you all the time. I didn't meet him often then. When I moved here he used to come now and again from Oxford. His old friend, Owen Barfield, brought him out here once or twice. And Warnie, his brother, came once. And once the David Cecils came at the same time. Usually it was for lunch, more usually a friendly call, perhaps unexpected. Lewis would go into the kitchen and hand the food through the hatch into the dining room. Once I said, "This is only lentil soup made from bacon water."

And he said, "Good! I like lentil soup made with boiled bacon water." He was very touching like that, very simple and useful. Once I gave Lewis several jars of marmalade to take home. I knew he liked marmalade.

When Jack (Lewis) brought his brother, Major "Warnie" Lewis, I asked Jack if I might query him about the first of his children's books,[7] *The Lion, the Witch and the Wardrobe.* Our conversation went like this:

PITTER:	In the land of Narnia, the witch makes it always winter and never Christmas?
LEWIS:	Yes.
PITTER:	Does she allow any foreign trade?
LEWIS:	She does not.
PITTER:	Am I allowed to postulate on the lines of Santa Claus with the tea tray?
LEWIS:	You are not.
PITTER:	Then where did all the materials for the good dinner the beavers gave come from?
LEWIS:	The beavers caught fish through holes in the ice.
PITTER:	Yes, the potatoes to go with them, the flour and sugar and oranges and milk for the children?
LEWIS:	I must refer you to a further study of the text.
MAJOR LEWIS:	Nonsense, Jack! You're stumped. And you know it.

The interview with Miss Pitter continued with her observation:

"I think Lewis really minded being stumped, just a little. It is one of the ways in which the Irish differ from us. I've noticed they tend not to like 'leg pulls.' I was in the position of, say, a small boy who is allowed to bowl to a great batsman, and get him out by lucky chance. But then, I am intensely practical, and have grown tons of food in my time. Lewis's hands were only good to write with; there was something a little abnormal about his thumbs. And although he was strong and burly, he was no gardener; but he could *make paths*. How symbolic this is!"

"Later, Miss Pitter, you did meet Mrs. Gresham, the woman Lewis married, didn't you?"

"Yes, once only."

"According to your correspondence in the Bodleian Library, that was on January 24, 1954—more than two years before Lewis married Mrs. Gresham. The three of you had lunch together at the Eastgate Hotel in Oxford—is that right?"

"Yes."

"What was she like? Was she normal or did she have a crutch or walking stick?"

"She was quite normal. Not ill, not that one could see."

"What was she like herself?"

"Don't ask me. I wrote it out and put it away in a safe place, not to be opened for fifty years or more."

"That was a sensible thing to do, Miss Pitter. Well, you had a pleasant little luncheon party together?"

"No. It was not pleasant. It was not. I can tell you that much."

"I see. Well, Miss Pitter, may I ask about all those letters from Lewis that you gave to the Bodleian Library—a volume about an inch thick—they must have been worth a fortune?"

"Yes, they were. I implored them not to tell me what they were worth. At that time Texas was paying almost anything for Lewis's letters. But you understand I couldn't take Lewis's letters to market."

"I understand perfectly. Now please tell me, Miss Pitter, Lewis says how disappointed he was when you went to Oxford and he wasn't there. And even after his marriage he still wrote to you."

"Yes, he did. And I wrote to Joy Lewis too. After that magical recovery I wrote to her from time to time; but I never heard from her."

"After she died you saw Lewis again. What was he like then?"

"He was the same old Lewis. He had suffered from that bone disease, osteoporosis; and he had to wear an awful 'straightjacket' because his bones were breaking down. It is a very painful disease, and it diminished his stature. He was rather slumped into himself. But his voice was still full and resonant. He was still a little mischievous and humorous too. And he said, 'Won't you take your hat off?' And I wouldn't because I thought my hair was in a mess. I did wish afterwards I had taken my hat off when he asked me. I felt mean. I didn't know it was to be the last time I saw him. The next day he wrote me a few lines, 'Your visit brought me great pleasure. . . .'I never saw him again."

— 15 —

The Fun of the Thing

A.J.P. Taylor

> *A.J.P. Taylor and Lewis were Fellows together at Magdalen College, Oxford, for about twenty years. Mr. Taylor still is an honorary Fellow with rooms near Lewis's old rooms. Mr. Taylor is a historian. A Lewis pupil assures me that historians of all views, some of whom disagree with Mr. Taylor, nevertheless regard him with great respect as one of the most eminent historical writers of his generation. Of his numerous books one of the finest is considered to be* The Origins of the Second World War. *He is also widely known as a broadcaster and lecturer. I called at his office and taped his remarks.*

Lewis and I walked round Addison's Walk. But in the summer he and I used to bathe at what was called The College Bathing Place. You are allowed to go there until 8:00 in the morning. At the other end of Addison's Walk you can go into the Cherwell River. Undergraduates had stopped doing this, but Lewis and I used to meet at about 7:30 in the morning, plunging into the Cherwell.

During the war I participated in the education program for the forces on Current Affairs and Lewis did it, of course, on religious education. He used to get mainly women audiences—ATS and WAAF. He was very popular with service women as a result of his talks about religion. We got a fee for this, and he and I agreed that as we were fully paid members of the College we would not accept this fee, but would put it into a special fund to be used to help the soldiers when they came back. Between us I think we earned about 10,000 pounds during the course of the war. It has been used ever since as a source of grants. Our idea was that it would be spent fairly soon; but some of it was kept for a long time. Lewis never talked about religion in the College. We didn't want to hear it for one thing. None of us was sympathetic to him, so he kept quiet. He often talked about literature and, in my opinion, he had adolescent tastes and adult gifts of appreciation. What he liked was what he called a "rattling good yarn." He didn't like Dickens much; it was great fun; but what he liked was the story. He sat next to me one day in the autumn and said,"I have had a wonderful summer; I have reread all Scott." That was the sort of book he liked. No interest in modern literature or modern poetry. He didn't approve of Hardy. He almost stopped with Tennyson. He liked Scott; he liked Stevenson; he liked anyone who could tell a good tale.

While teaching English literature at Magdalen, Lewis helped in the history school by teaching political theory. He took the history students. His lectures covered Rousseau and Aristotle, et. al. He loved doing this. He loved playing with ideas. He had a very, very quick mind and it could be a destructive mind, too. He never liked college administration. He became vice-president, which is a two-year office, and after one year he said he couldn't do it any more.

After the war, when people were coming back to their positions, there was a young man for whom there was no position. His friends wanted to get him back into the College. They suggested that the soldiers coming back would be very rowdy—this was quite untrue; they were most orderly—and that we ought to have a fellow who would simply keep order. He would be paid full-time for doing nothing but keeping order. Some of us were very much against this. We realized it was just a job to keep this young man in. We didn't need such a person, but we were in the minority and we thought we hadn't a hope. When the committee met, Lewis was present and, taking no notice, he was dozing off and on. He would write letters all through committee meetings because he didn't care about them in the slightest, but on this day, he suddenly woke up and said in his richest voice: "President, will this post be advertised?"

And the President said, "Oh, no; we have an excellent man for it."

"Oh, but President," said Lewis, "it is a *plum*. Two thousand pounds a year for doing nothing. It is the greatest plum I have ever known. I think if it is advertised I shall apply for it. I should like such a plum."

And this word "plum" got bigger and bigger and the President got more and more annoyed, and people laughed more and more, and the proposal was completely defeated.

Afterwards I told Lewis, "You saved us. You realize this was a corrupt job and we had no means of throwing it out."

"Oh," he said, "I had no idea. I just thought it was a plum."

You ask about Lewis and music, Mr. Schofield. Well, in my opinion he had no musical sense at all. Lewis didn't know anything about music. But he adored Wagner's Ring Cycle of operas. Only Wagner, because these are fairy tales rather like Lewis's you see? He used to go to Covent Garden nearly every year only to Wagner. And the music meant nothing to him whatsoever. Nor did opera. The music didn't go. In fact he once said to me, 'Wagner's operas would be much better without the music!" He wanted the story. Oh, yes, I knew Lewis well. He and I joined the Home Guard on the very same day it was made in the summer of 1940. And as soon as the Battle of Britain was over Lewis said to me, "We are not going to be invaded so I am not going to stay in the Home Guard." So he and I then resigned.

(Editor's note: I asked Mr. Taylor if he would please comment on a few statements of Lewis's. One of these involved Lord Macaulay, who, according to *Pear's Cyclopaedia,* "was the most brilliant historian of the Victorian era." Lord Macaulay, according to Lewis, however, *". . . is a humbug—a vulgar, shallow, self-satisfied mind, absolutely inaccessible to the complexities and delicacies of the real world. He has the journalist's air of being a specialist in everything, of taking all points of view, and being always on the side of the angels; he merely annoys a reader who has had the least experience of* knowing *things, of what knowing is like. There is not two-pence worth of real thought or real nobility in him. But he isn't dull."*[1])

TAYLOR (laughing): Both are true. Macaulay was a great historian and he still is wonderfully readable. But it is also true that he had a very shallow mind. I think Lewis is nearer the truth.[2]

Lewis wrote, *"War is caused by pride. Greed will make a man want more money for a better house, and so forth, but only up to a point. What makes a man or a nation demand more and more, to be richer and more powerful than others, is pride. What prompts a beautiful woman to spread misery by attracting admirers wherever she goes? Pride again. Pride is the chief cause of misery in every family and nation since the world began."*

TAYLOR: Well, there is something of pride in Lewis too. A friend of mine went to a religious gathering. A lot of people who either talked about religion or were known as religious figures, were present. Lewis was one. Another was the well known Roman Catholic, Father Martin D'Arcy. And while they were talking, Father D'Arcy, without knowing who he was referring to, said to a friend, "Who is that man in the corner showing off?" That was Lewis.

Lewis wrote, *"The side of me which longs . . . to be approved as a writer, is not the side . . . that is really worth much. . . . A man must reach the stage of not caring two straws about his own status . . . . The only thing . . . to do is absolutely to* kill *the part of you that wants success."*[3]

TAYLOR: You see! He did it once or twice.

Lewis wrote, *"It is not your business to succeed (no one can be sure of that) but to do right: when you have done so, the rest lies with God . . . ."*[4]

TAYLOR: I don't think Lewis believed that.[5]

Lewis wrote, *"Who knows . . . what will in the end reach the ear of humanity? The successes of our own age may be speedily forgotten: some poem scribbled in pencil on the fly leaf of a schoolbook may survive and be read and be an influence when English is a dead language . . . . I am sure that some are born to write as trees are born to bear leaves: for these, writing is a necessary mode of their own development. If the impulse to write survives the hope of success, then one is among these. If not, then the impulse was at best only pardonable vanity . . . . I think we may depend upon it that endless and devoted work on an object to which a man feels seriously impelled will tell* somewhere or other: himself or others, in this world or others, will reap a harvest exactly proportional to the output."[6]

TAYLOR: Right! *That* I think he did believe.

Lewis wrote, *"Ambition! We must be careful what we mean by it. If it means the desire to get ahead of other people—which is what I think it does mean—then it is bad. If it means simply wanting to do a thing well, then it is good. It isn't wrong for an actor to want to act his part as well as it can possibly be acted, but the wish to have his name in bigger type than the other actors is a bad one . . . . What we call 'ambition' usually means the wish to be more conspicuous or more successful than someone else. It is this competitive element in it that is bad. It is perfectly reasonable to want to dance well or to look nice. But when the dominant wish is to dance better or look nicer than the others—when you begin to feel that if the others danced as well as you or looked as nice as you, that would take the fun out of it—then you are doing wrong.*[7]

Finally, I showed Mr. Taylor a statement about Lewis which one of his pupils, Norman Bradshaw, had given me:

> Lewis liked to demolish an opponent's argument. He liked to win. When he was with friends, the Inklings, for instance, I imagine he was hearty and warm, hail fellow well met. But quite often during or after dinner with people a point might crop up in conversation. Lewis would take up the argument and knock the other chap as flat as a house of cards. There was nothing left for him to say. He was out and speechless. And Lewis would sit back and take another sip of port. And that man might well have been, later, the very one whose good word could have tipped the scales for a professorship for Lewis.

Mr. Taylor responded, Yes. That is very good. I'd say he could never resist an argument. I don't think he wanted to score. It was the fun of the thing. That's what he did it for. If he had an idea in his head he would like to take it up. It never crossed his mind that the other chap would be hurt.

— 16 —

Observations of a Magdalen Don

Sir David Hunt

Colonel Sir David Hunt served in various Diplomatic Service posts abroad, and also at No. 10 Downing Street where he was private secretary to Prime Minister Attlee and Prime Minister Churchill. His own two books are: A Don at War *and* On the Spot. *Sometimes he reviewed Lewis's books for* The Times Literary Supplement. *Since 1978 he has been editor of* The Times Yearbook of World Affairs. *He is chairman of the board of governors of the Commonwealth Institute.*

My qualifications for writing about Lewis are not great. I could be described as an acquaintance—and an admirer—rather than a friend. The acquaintanceship began in the autumn of 1937 when I was elected to a fellowship at Magdalen that lasted only a little over two years because I joined the Army at the end of 1939 and was posted overseas in May, 1940. I never saw him again after that as I served abroad continuously until 1947. My memories are imprecise but affectionate, an emotion which has been strengthened by the pleasure which his books on literary criticism have given me. I bought each one as it came out and constantly reread them. I don't, on the other hand, care much for his stories or apologetic works, although some of his papers for the Socratic Club are powerful and entertaining specimens of polemic.

In appearance he was very much the typical don of the thirties. He was genial and rubicund sub-genus, rather than the dessicated. We met constantly because he spent most of his time in college, as I did; we would be thrown together at dinner in hall, then afterwards in the common room to take port and then again in the smoking room where he usually would sit, talking over a glass of whiskey until about 10:00. I knew his reputation as a most popular lecturer in the English faculty but had never heard him; I read *Literae Humaniores* (Classics, Philosophy and Ancient History), better known as "Greats," and was at the time engaged in Greek archaeology, which involved spending my summers in Greece. Lewis had also read "Greats": I think he would have preferred to teach in that faculty but took a post in English literature instead because one became available. His love for classical literature was very strong and he had a thorough knowledge of it. His conversations with me were mainly on subjects connected with it, though he would very civilly draw me out on the latest news on Greek archaeology, both because he was interested and also because he was a good-natured and polite man who liked to encourage people to talk on their own subjects. He was always affable to younger persons and never patronizing; I was the junior fellow and only twenty-three at the time I was elected.

I don't remember Lewis ever speaking at a College meeting. He took hardly any interest in academic politics, nor in national politics, although Magdalen was noted for the active part it played in the former and 1937-1939 were years which saw passionate debate over the chances of war or peace than any other period in my lifetime.

What left a deeper impression than my own conversations with him was listening to him talking in the smoking room with his particular friends. The greatest of these, I think, was J.R.R. Tolkien, who was a frequent visitor. Tolkien, whom I knew only slightly, was a drier type. They were both keen philologists, with a particular interest in Nordic languages. They used to enjoy making up imaginary Indo-European languages on the basis of assuming, for example, that one or another of the laws philologists have discovered had never existed. Another philologist, also a fellow of Magdalen, was Charles Talbot Onions, who had served on the team that compiled the great *Oxford English Dictionary*. Onions had a passion for words, and especially for etymologies; it was a pleasure to hear the two together because they would chat loudly, amusingly and always with knowledge. Another friend was R.H. Chapman, the editor of Johnson and Jane Austen, and formerly of the Oxford University Press.

It was during this period that Lewis's first important book, *The Allegory of Love,* came out. Up till then I think he had passed for a fairly run-of-the-mill don and its reception was all the more striking. It was instantly recognized as a work of genius. G.M. Young wrote in a review: "Anyone can see that Mr. Lewis has written a good book: learned, penetrating and eloquent. My own feeling is that he has written a great book, in the tradition of Ker's *Epic and Romance* and Bradley's *Shakespearean Tragedy"* (reprinted *Daylight and Champaign,* Jonathan Cape Ltd., London, 1937). *The Allegory of Love* is the only book of his that I ever discussed with him, though I can't remember anything of the discussion beyond expressing my own admiration. I still think very highly of it, though my favorite is his *English Literature in the Sixteenth Century,* especially the first chapter. This is the chapter in which he told Nevill Coghill that he had proved the Renaissance never happened in England or, if it did, it was not of much importance. I find it very convincing. In second place I would put *A Preface to Paradise Lost* which is also an admirable introduction to epic poetry in general. He is especially profound on Homer. And a final word for *The Discarded Image,* so valuable for our understanding of medieval and renaissance literature.

Nothing very personal so far, you may say. I'll end with a remark I heard him make in the smoking room. He was telling Chapman about a pupil whose tastes ran to contemporary poetry (his did not) and whom he quoted as saying that poetry could be written on any subject: the ostensible subject was of no importance, what counted was the technique. "How immensely you must admire Kipling's poetry," was what he had replied. A just remark: Kipling's ideas may be unattractive but no one can deny he was a superb technician. Lewis himself disliked Kipling as a pagan, and for other reasons, though he observes acutely "some poems could not, on internal evidence alone, be distinguished from Christian work." There is an acute and understanding chapter on Kipling in *They Asked for a Paper* to which, in conclusion, I commend your attention.

— 17 —

The Mystery

Malcolm Muggeridge

Mr. Muggeridge, a distinguished English journalist and author of numerous books, is also a well-known television personality on both sides of the Atlantic. He lives in a modest house in Sussex. I visited him there and taped his remarks.

"Though one way or another C.S. Lewis wrote quite a lot about himself, and has been much written about, he has remained a somewhat inscrutable figure—at least to me. Nor can it be said that Roger Lancelyn Green and Walter Hooper, in their otherwise excellent biographical study,[1] succeed in wholly dispelling this inscrutability. They are perhaps too conscientious, too careful, too respectful, to get under Lewis's guard and penetrate his defences."[2] So wrote Malcolm Muggeridge in his review of the Lewis biography.

"What is it, Mr. Muggeridge," I asked, "that you find inscrutable about Lewis?"

"Well, it is in his life. Something was missing. I felt something inscrutable did not come out in the book. There is something strange in him that I don't fully understand. I mean, I feel in his life there is an element of mystery."

"Would you feel there was any mystery about—say, Harold Macmillan, the former prime minister?"

"No, no mystery about him."

"Or Lord Attlee, the old Labour leader?"

127

"No, no mystery about Clem Attlee."

"Well, what is it about Lewis?"

"Something hasn't come out. I think it has to do with his attitude toward women and sex, some evasion he is hiding from us. I think he was probably a very deeply sensual man; and he fought to put it away from him. It gives you something one doesn't quite understand. I don't know whether or not I am right. That is why it is a mystery."

"You've struck a point there, Mr. Muggeridge, I do agree, a very tender spot. A man[3] on the radio said Lewis himself always said he was afraid of sexuality in the flesh, and that when he had women as pupils he had great difficulty in keeping his hands off them. This man—I think his name was Kark—said it seemed very strange to him. And I know another man, Norman Bradshaw,[4] a pupil of Lewis's—he told me the matter of Lewis and sex was a mystery to him too. He said it was a standing joke at Magdalen whenever a woman came on the College grounds, Lewis would run as fast as his legs would take him to his room and lock the door. However exaggerated that may be, it is odd."

"Yes, it is," said Mr. Muggeridge, "as long as he didn't take her in."

"But I think he did have a prejudice against women. It slips out sometimes. For instance, he says Eve is the mother of all corrupting *female* novelists.[5] Why pick on females? There are quite as many corrupting male novelists, possibly more. Again, he refers to marriage as the "fatal tomb of all lively and interesting men."[6] And certainly both Lewis brothers were reluctant to join the ladies that evening at Hugo Dyson's.[7] I agree with you about the prejudice, Mr. Muggeridge, and his shying away from women. But it's not strange or mysterious to me."

"It's not?"

"No. It all seems logical to me, Mr. Muggeridge. I'd say the root of the matter is that he was only nine years old when he lost his mother. That's a pretty tough one to start with. And he had no sisters. And he had a difficult father. That makes an unbalanced background. So little feminine companionship. And, as he grew up, he had other impediments. Women like good looks. Well, he was not exactly a Romeo to look at. Women like athletes. He wasn't any good at sports. Major Lewis told me that himself. It seems to me perfectly logical that he would shy away from girls—and prefer Homer. Instead of the enchantment of pretty girls he had the enchantment of great books most of us never reach in a lifetime. For most adolescents great moments occur when certain girls say, 'I'd love to have the next dance!' For Lewis, at sixteen, great moments occurred in the Surrey countryside, when he opened parcels from London, cheap editions of Milton and Spenser. He had compensations. But he missed the happy integration of the sexes. I don't know, Mr. Muggeridge. Of course I don't know. I'm only guessing. But I think that's how the prejudice began. A lopsided family. Not his fault at all. Now please tell me something about his work, Mr. Muggeridge. What do you think of it? What do you think is the best of *Mere Christianity*?[8] Personally I prefer those few pages on pride."

"Yes. A fine chapter, that. Very fine on pride, I quite agree. But the whole book is a brilliant piece of exposition. I like *The Problem of Pain*[9] too. But I'd say the one that caught my interest most is *The Screwtape Letters*.[10] I think he has got a very profound point that the devil has a much better opportunity with sentimental good people than with vicious people. He has a much better opening. He gets someone like Mrs. Roosevelt. And he can really make hay with that. Lewis saw this. A lot of people don't."

"Would you say that Lewis was a fortunate encounter for you, Mr. Muggeridge?"

"Yes, for me Lewis was a fortunate encounter because he had this very clear mind. And remember that I don't like universities or dons. I mean temperamentally I don't like them. The fact that Lewis was so completely a don that his approach to the thing was the approach of a don; and his joking, his facetiousness, is a don's facetiousness. You see what I mean. And there is a lack of sympathy there. But as I read him I am overwhelmed by the clarity of his mind, and his sincerity, the total sincerity and honesty of his thoughts and beliefs. That's the point. But as a don, as a man who has lived all his life in this University—well, I was at Cambridge. I very much disliked it as a place. I couldn't stand these dons. I hated Cambridge."

"You hated Cambridge!"

"Yes, I hated it. I don't like universities at all. So my admiration for Lewis is, in a sense, won from me reluctantly. It is a measure of how good he is that he gets that. Because he loved Oxford and he was a don of dons, wasn't he? And, you know, they irritate me. And scholarship I haven't much opinion of, either. I think it is a kind of second-rate activity. But still he wins me in spite of all that, because of the wonderful clarity and the genuiness and true humility he achieved. I think no one has presented the Christian faith to the twentieth century mind as clearly as he has."

— 18 —

Impact

Stephen Schofield

Lewis irked some people.

A distinguished author and one of his close friends in Oxford, J.R.R. Tolkien, disapproved of his work. In the Narnian tales he hated the heavy theological allegory. He thought Lewis had taken a bit of the myth and rendered it commonplace. Nor did he approve of *That Hideous Strength.* "Tripish, I fear," said Tolkien.[1]

A sharper critic is Alistair Cooke, the author and broadcaster who hosts "Masterpiece Theatre." He says Lewis's explanation of every problem comes out with a patness that murders the points it pretends to clarify; he muddles millions.[2] "It was really the war," said Mr. Cooke, "that pitchforked Lewis into the limelight."[3]

And Victor Yarros wrote in *The American Freeman,* "C.S. Lewis, the paradox-monger and word-juggler will surely meet his match one of these days and be subjected to a severe debunking operation. He is asking for it. Oh, for a Huxley or a Heine to expose his tricks and call his bluffs!"[4]

Lewis has written at least one error. This is well-noted by his brother, Major Warren Lewis. He says that Lewis's description of school life is absurdly exaggerated; that he induced his brother to admit this; and that this was the only occasion he ever induced Lewis to admit he had been wrong.[5]

Another setback occurred at the hands—or rather the voice—of a woman, Miss—now Professor—G.E.M. Anscombe, the well-known philosopher. At a Socratic Club meeting in Oxford, in 1948, she took

Lewis on and beat him, according to some who attended, though others in the audience affirm that Lewis won. In any case Lewis was sufficiently shaken to revise chapter three of *Miracles*[6] before it was reprinted in paperback in 1960.

Apart from these contradictions, his work appears to be firm and far-reaching in effect, sometimes in unusual people. One is Charles Colson, a leading conspirator of the Watergate scandal. Colson, President Nixon's special counsel, was one of three or four men who could walk in and out of the Oval Office to advise the President on various decisions. He had arrived. When he and Nixon and Bob Haldeman, three men alone in a private office, watched the 1972 landslide returns piling in on election night, he expected elation. Instead he felt an inner emptiness and deadness which persisted for some months. He was too smart to attend the meetings John Dean testified about. If something was not quite right at the White House, Colson would look the other way and not be part of it. But when he had been queried by Congressional committees and grand juries, and when he could not get out of a car without a microphone being thrust in front of him, he began to think he was not as smart as he had thought he was. He had never seen so many people so set against each other. Washington seemed to be seething with hatred. The only relief in the midst of it all came to him in the form of a concerned friend named Philips. On the warm evening of August 12, 1973, on the porch of his own home, Philips read to Colson a chapter from Lewis's *Mere Christianity:* how pride has been the chief cause of misery since the world began, setting one man against another. Colson recognized the source of the emptiness and deadness: how he had tried all his life to prove to his family, to his friends, and most of all to himself, how smart he was. As Philips read Colson felt a burning sensation; his face flushed. The words went straight into him. He felt exposed, his defenses gone. He felt he was the very man Lewis was writing about. When Philips offered him the book, Colson accepted it without demur. But he was not going to let Philips think it could mean much to *him,* an ex-Marine captain, presidential confidant, White House hatchet man, the one the press corps called the toughest of the Nixon tough guys. Outside, ready to start his car, Colson found the tears welling up and he had difficulty in getting the keys into the ignition. He managed to get going, slowly, and set off on a long drive to the Maine coast. His mind turned to courts. How thankful he was he had never had to oppose Lewis in court. Such clarity and logic! Arriving at the Maine coast, Colson did what he used to do as a lawyer, preparing a case for court. He tabled the facts. Out came his little yellow pad and a pencil. While his world was collapsing about him, all in darkness, it seemed, his friends being indicted and he himself awaiting indictment, for days he made notes from that little book Philips had given him. Underscored and dog-eared, its pages falling out, it fostered his faith. Back in Washington, when it was quietly announced in the White House press room one morning, that tough-guy Colson had "gone religious" and was indeed attending a prayer breakfast, pandemonium broke out among the reporters. There was no other story out of the White House that day. The telephone started ringing. Incredulous reporters called Colson for confirmation. "Would you repeat that please . . . a little more slowly . . . ." He confirmed it. Over the telephone he could hear the laughter in the newsrooms. Jokes and cartoons appeared in papers across the country. One showed Colson in a monk's habit, kneeling in front of the White House; it was headed, "Repent." Another depicted Nixon looking out and saying, "Colson's gone religious! Quick! Call Billy Graham." Old friends advised Colson, "Cut it out, Chuck. You're making a fool of yourself." From others, complete strangers in various parts of the country, Colson received hundreds of warmhearted letters. One affected him deeply: ". . . I am a staff sergeant in the US Air Force and for nineteen years I have been trying to find myself. I went to church on some occasions; but the pastors didn't reach me. After reading an article on you—it has helped me more than anything. It is now Christmas morning. I am usually drunk or trying to get drunk. But now I am watching the children open their presents and thinking about going to church instead of getting drunk. I didn't even buy any booze this year. I feel free within myself this morning and I pray God may help both of us in our efforts. God's blessing on you. (Signed) A--- B---, Staff Sergeant." A staff sergeant! In eleven years with the government, of all the executive letters Colson had written and all of the things he had done which he thought had changed the lives of millions, he could not think of a single life he had changed for the better. And here was a staff sergeant showing him what life could mean. Why, he had a staff sergeant drive his limousine to the

White House; colonels would salute; generals would wait to see him. Colson changed. His views and feeling changed, especially after serving seven months in prison.

He has told the essence of all this many times, face to face with prisoners in England and Japan, as well as in the U.S. and Canada. In 1982 in Yokohama, Japan, he told prisoners "how Jesus had made him realize his greatest sin, pride, which was the center of his life; and how He changed him and caused him to be born again." In the course of these talks he often mentions Lewis's *Mere Christianity* which "induced him to kneel before the Lord."[7] Into auras of gloom and despair, he brings hope. A long list of prisons await his presence. And his two books, *Born Again* and *Life Sentence*,[8] have been translated into several languages.

One day a woman spoke to the Reverend Dr. Chad Walsh of Beloit College, Wisconsin. In great excitement she told him of a book she had just read, *Perelandra*.[9] She lent it to him. He read it right through, quickly; and apart from the sheer beauty of the book, he said later, that he was transported and shaken as he never had been before. He followed it up by reading everything he could find by Lewis, spent a summer in Oxford visiting Lewis and gathering material for a book, despite Lewis's discouraging the idea (as he usually did discourage anyone wanting to write about him). The result was *C.S. Lewis: Apostle to the Skeptics*.[10] This is still considered to be one of the best books on Lewis. He believes Lewis's impact on the religious thought and imagination of America has been rarely, if ever, equaled by any other modern writer. Dr. Walsh has now written another book, *The Literary Legacy of C.S. Lewis*,[11] a major analysis of the historical and intellectual influences that shaped Lewis's literary sensibility. In a separate article Dr. Walsh had predicted a decline in Lewis's popularity. He was wrong. And in his new book he admits he was wrong. Lewis, he says, is "going through the roof."

Another English teacher, Dr. Clyde Kilby of Wheaton College, Illinois, picked up a copy of *Broadcast Talks*[12] one morning in the College bookshop. It shook him. What shook him was the impression of a man who had won a battle, inside and deep, against pose, expedience, and the ever-so-little lie and wished with all his heart to honor truth in every idea passing through his mind. He read everything Lewis wrote, arranged courses using his books, visited Oxford to see him, returned to England several times, and established a Collection at Wheaton honoring Lewis and other writers such as George MacDonald and J.R.R. Tolkien, who were either close friends of his or strong influences. The Collection includes hundreds of Lewis's letters, drawings, manuscripts; his desk and table; and the actual wardrobe which inspired the first of the Narnian tales, *The Lion, the Witch and the Wardrobe.* Dr. Kilby has produced six books about Lewis.[13]

What impresses the learned? Well, T.S. Eliot's favorite book of Lewis's was *A Preface to Paradise Lost.*[14] This sells at the rate of about 1,500 copies a year.[15] One reason, a school inspector informs me, is that it is on the sixth form syllabus for English schools. Here is a sample of it:

> Satan is the best drawn of Milton's characters. The reason is not far to find . . . . To make a character worse than oneself it is only necessary to release imaginatively from control . . . some of the bad passions which, in real life, are always straining at the leash; the Satan . . . within each of us is always there and only too ready, the moment the leash is slipped, to come out and have in our books that holiday we try to deny them in our lives. But if you try to draw a character better than yourself, all you can do is to take the best moments you have had and to imagine them prolonged and more consistently embodied in action . . . . It is in their 'good' characters that novelists make, unawares, their most shocking self-revelations.[16]

Even in Britain, where Lewis has long since passed out of fashion, the annual sale of 1,500 copies of this book is not so surprising. A similar annual sale is current in the US.

Part of Lewis's impact is in letters to unsolicited correspondents who descended upon him in staggering numbers. The letters[17] published by his brother contain a mere fraction of his output. His adoptive mother, Mrs. Moore, received scores of letters from him; she burned them all.[18] In the Bodleian Library in Oxford are at least five volumes, each about eighteen by twelve inches, and one inch thick, of unpublished letters, nearly all handwritten and beautifully preserved.

Many offer solutions to problems. Although he enjoyed writing books, he did not enjoy advising "Mrs. Whosis of Idaho" how to cope with an unfaithful husband. And he must have written hundreds of such letters. The most recent lot to be published are the 225 letters to his old friend Arthur Greeves.[19]

One woman in Washington, D.C., wrote to Lewis almost monthly for more than ten years, rarely omitting her woes—her fall, cold, sore throat; operation, rheumatism, sinus headaches; neuralgia, poverty, hives; dental trouble, cat trouble, mumps; earache, heart trouble, Asian flu; fear of an operation, bad nights, expenses, and mental debility. Her letters were long. And Lewis, burdened with lectures, tutoring, papers to mark, a difficult household to manage and his own writing which a vast public was crying for, had his American publishers send her a monthly allowance, subsequently increased, and answered nearly every letter in his own hand, full of sympathy and warmth, until he himself was dying in an Oxford hospital.[20] Towards the end he told her that, after all, neither of them would live much longer, and then, he said, it will be fun to meet (in heaven).[21]

I asked W.H. Lewis about such letters, and he said, "Yes, Jack's capacity for writing to all sorts of people with so many kinds of problems was astonishing, as was the care with which he turned from his own heavy work to deal with each. I acted as his private secretary for many years, and looking back, I am surprised at the small number of letters he let me draft for his signature—hardly any except those dealing with trivialities."[22]

During the war a frustrated U.S. serviceman wrote an angry letter to Lewis. He received a long and charitable reply which made him see very clearly the tangled state of his own life. He is now Professor Paul L. Holmer of Yale University and author of *C.S. Lewis: The Shape of His Faith and Thought.*[23] He says Lewis makes us see things anew, and see things we had never seen before, and want what we have never wanted before—humility, candor, contentment—inducing us to grow up naturally and quickly; not by imposing a moral authority, but indirectly, by suggesting that the stake is high for each person, and each one is full of glorious possibilities.

Lewis became involved with Sheldon and Jean Vanauken, a young American pagan couple who came to Oxford as students. They were extraordinarily in love with each other, and with music and books and Oxford and its environs. At the suggestion of friends, the Vanaukens dipped into Lewis's books, and to their astonishment wound up as converts and personal friends of Lewis's. Sheldon Vanauken later became an English teacher at Lynchburg College, Virginia, and there—while still in their thirties—Jean unexpectedly died, probably from a virus. (Even a post-mortem did not disclose the cause.) Vanauken said to himself: I must not falter. And he prayed. Lewis, by means of long letters, proved to be the one friend he could grip in the dark and in the daylight. And it was one particular letter from Lewis that enabled him to make sense out of his wife's death, and his own life, and prompted him to write a complete account of his love for Jean and Lewis. The consequent book,[24] containing twenty-six letters from Lewis, reveals what is probably the most powerful, known impact Lewis had on any Oxford student. The fact that it has sold more than 100,000 copies in hardback, and that its paperback sales are expected to reach a million, is not surprising.

At present Lewis ranks fifth among popular children's writers. First are the books of Enid Blyton; then Louisa Alcott's *Little Women;* Anna Sewell's *Black Beauty;* Robert L. Stevenson's *Treasure Island;* and C.S. Lewis's *The Lion, the Witch and the Wardrobe.*

His impact in other countries is varied. A current decade of index translatoniums reveal that his books sell in Scandinavian and European countries, chiefly in Germany, and occasionally in Japan and Israel. The Narnian tales, *The Screwtape Letters, The Problem of Pain, The Great Divorce, Mere Christianity, Surprised by Joy, Reflections on the Psalms, The Worlds's Last Night and Other Essays,* would seem to be the most popular, roughly in that order.

Some of his books have sold in France. The French intelligentsia is larger than the British, probably because France has more universities.[25] But the old hostility between the French and English impedes the sale of English books in France. In the preface to the French editions, the main point Lewis mentions is this:

> Because I have been an atheist for a long time I have realized
> one point which others, born faithful, perhaps cannot see.
> In spite of divisions, I recognized the same undeniable
> aroma permeating the work of Dante, Bunyan, Thomas
> Aquinas or William Law.[26]

In all North America, oddly enough, it was not at Princeton University, or Harvard or Yale, or even Toronto, that someone had the perception to honor Lewis. As early as 1952, it was Quebec's French-Canadian University of Laval that conferred on him an honorary degree. An American monk, Brother Stanislas, remarks, "I am not a great Lewis enthusiast. But I do enjoy some of his works, above all, the Narnian Chronicles. I've read them about three times in the last three years, and they have been for me the most spiritual books I have read in my sixteen years as a monk. They are just chuck-full of insights into who God is, who we are, and how we relate to God and to one another. And it is all presented in such a delightful and imaginative way that it really goes deep into your heart and whole being. Quite a few of us Trappists are Narnians for life."[27] Perhaps this explains why French publishers show such interest in Lewis. For certainly a dozen books produced by five French publishers is remarkable for a British writer.

What is believed to be the first and only book about Lewis that is actually written in French by a Frenchman is *The Life and Works of David Lindsay* by Bernard Sellin.[28] Lewis is much involved here because, as he himself mentions to an American scholar, "The real father of my planet books is David Lindsay's *Voyage to Arcturus,* which you will also revel in if you don't know it . . . . It was Lindsay who first gave me the idea that 'scientification' could be combined with 'supernatural' appeal."[29]

Again, he writes to his friend Ruth Pitter, the poet, *"Voyage to Arcturus* is not the parody of *Perelandra* but its father. It was published, a dead failure, about 25 years ago. Now that the author is dead it is suddenly leaping into fame: but I am one of the old guard who had treasured a second-hand copy before anyone had ever heard of it. From Lindsay I first learnt what other planets in fiction are really good for: spiritual adventures. Only they can satisfy the craving which sends our imagination off the earth."[30]

In Germany, until recently, there has been little interest in C.S. Lewis. On June 20, 1983, however, Dr. Gisbert Kranz communicated to the editor, "In Germany the Lewis boom has at last taken hold. More than thirty Lewis titles are now in German in the bookstores, many in inexpensive pocket editions, and are selling like cakes. The *Inklings-Gesellschaft für Literatur and Äesthetic* was founded in May 1983. The periodical of this society is the *Inklings-Jahrbuch*. The aim of this periodical and of our society is scholarly investigation into the works of C.S. Lewis, J.R.R. Tolkien, and Charles Williams. We celebrate the twentieth anniversary of C.S. Lewis's death at Aachen from November 21 to November 26, 1983 by a C.S. Lewis exhibition, a Tolkien exhibition, and nine lectures by experts from London, Brighton, Wien, Frankfurt, Duisburg and Marburg."

In Switzerland the title used for *Beyond Personality* is: "To Be or Not to Be," perhaps unwittingly Shakespearean? And in Holland, *The Problem of Pain* is called "God's Megaphone." These are apt titles. Of late, *The Screwtape Letters* and *Screwtape Proposes a Toast* have been published in Spanish as *Cartas del Diablo a Su Sobrino.*"[31]

"Lewis is pretty popular in Japan," reports Naoyuki Yagyu, Professor of English at Yokohama's Kanto Gakuin University. "I have translated into Japanese his *Miracles, Mere Christianity* and *The Great Divorce*. Others available in Japanese include all of the Narnian tales; the three science fiction works; *The Allegory of Love; The Problem of Pain; Surprised by Joy; A Grief Observed; Experiment in Criticism; Letters to Malcolm; The Screwtape Letters; Reflections on the Psalms; The Four Loves; The Weight of Glory,* and several other essays; and Arnott's *Secret Country of C.S. Lewis.* You ask me my own impressions of Lewis's books? He is my spiritual mentor. I owe him so much; it is impossible to write my impressions in a letter or two."

The first book about Lewis in Japanese, by a Japanese, is *The Land of Narnia Isn't Very Far* by Nozumu Yagyu, a younger brother of Naoyuki's. It is concerned chiefly with the Narnian tales and the science fiction trilogy. It has received favorable reviews and is selling well at present (1982). Another one in Japanese is being written by Naoyuki Yagyu, to be entitled *C.S. Lewis: His Faith and Achievements.*

In China, Paul Clasper is a senior lecturer at the Chinese University of Hong Kong. Once in 1977 he was invited to speak at a neighboring college on the mainland, The Lutheran Seminary in Shatin. He traveled by ferry and train, and when he arrived, deep in the mountains by some rice fields and a clump of golden bamboos, he felt as though he was in the interior of China. He spoke. A discussion followed. One of the students said that only recently had he come to appreciate his Chinese heritage in religion. What, Mr. Clasper enquired, had helped him most?

Very quickly, the student replied, "The writings of C.S. Lewis." Other students nodded and smiled and said that they had had the same experience. Mr. Clasper was amazed. After the discussion, trudging back through the bamboo and rice fields to the railway station, he felt a surge of gratitude for the disciplined mind of the professor who enlightened Asians as well as Westerners. *The Screwtape Letters,* he learned, had been translated into Chinese.[32]

One impact that is little known is the dramatization of *The Screwtape Letters,* no easy task. In 1959, during the run of his play "Heloise" in New York, James Forsyth was asked by the Dramatic Publishing Company to dramatize *The Screwtape Letters.* As he was about to return to England he agreed to approach Dr. Lewis himself to obtain full professional rights. Reports from Geoffrey Bles and Curtis Brown, who acted as Lewis's Literary Agents, were that Dr. Lewis was not keen on the book being dramatized.

Forsyth approached Lewis by letter. The response was cautious but from the first Lewis's attitude was helpful, courteous and kind. To talk the matter over he invited Mr. and Mrs. Forsyth to come to tea one afternoon. The Forsyths drove over from Sussex to Oxford; when they were half-way there Mrs. Forsyth telephoned to say that they had been held up and would be a bit late. Mrs. Lewis, who answered the telephone, was very peremptory: "You must be on time," she said. When the Forsyths arrived, however, Dr. and Mrs. Lewis were most friendly and they all sat down to tea. In visiting the eminent and the exceptionally intelligent, one is apt to feel small and overawed in their presence. The guests experienced no such feelings in the presence of Lewis. As Forsyth had, as yet, written nothing but notes, he had to do most of the talking; explaining what he planned to do with *Screwtape.*

After tea, Mrs. Lewis picked up a shotgun* standing in a corner of the room and led the surprised Mrs. Forsyth into the garden—quite a large garden—with a high close-boarded fence around it. She said a lot of houses had been built in the area and sometimes young neighbors climbed over the fence into their garden. She was annoyed that her husband should be disturbed and used the gun for frightening them off!

---

* This shotgun, leaning against the wall, is plainly visible in a photograph of Lewis taken by Dr. Militza Zernov. The photograph is used on page one of the July 1978 *Lamp-Post* of The Southern California C.S. Lewis Society.

While the ladies toured the garden the gentlemen cleared the table and continued the discussion. Lewis seemed interested and amused by Forsyth's approach to the proposed play. They repaired to the kitchen to wash the dishes. Sloshing hot water with a dishmop in the sink, Lewis said, "All right; treat the story in your own way; but why not use another name, another title? Then you don't have to pay me anything." He was quite unconcerned about copyright, or royalties coming to him; but this suggestion Forsyth could not accept; nor were the agents involved likely to agree. His idea was to call the play *"Dear Wormwood."* Lewis made no objection to this. "But" said Lewis, "you will have trouble. Doing anything with the Devil you are sure to have trouble." Then, with a twinkle in his eye, he added, "one thing the Devil can't stand is humor." He said this sympathetically but as a serious warning. The ladies returned from the garden (without a shot having been fired!). Mrs. Lewis put the gun back in the corner. The Forsyths left.

Forsyth wrote the draft of the play *Dear Wormwood* and sent the script to Lewis asking for comment or, if he wished, could he and Mrs. Lewis accept a return visit to Sussex or should the Forsyths come again to the Lewis home in Headington? Lewis said he could not leave home. And so again, in June 1960, Forsyth visited the Kilns, this time alone. When he arrived he realized he should not have been allowed to come; that it was extraordinarily considerate of Lewis to have let him come. Mrs. Lewis was gravely ill. Lewis himself, calm but obviously perturbed, inferred that her illness would be fatal. Despite this, he remarked "Let's drop the 'doctor' and 'mister' and get down to discussion of the work in hand." It was a useful talk which left Forsyth free to go ahead to complete the play. After some months he was able to send the full script to Lewis. The reply was "Congratulations. You have done it! I was uneasy about the conversion of *Wormwood,* but I found myself very moved when it happened."

It was not until two years after Lewis's death, in 1965, that plans to produce the play were completed. It opened in Brighton to—"Dear Wormwood is riotously funny" and toured Oxford, Golders Green and Hull. But trouble began early—as Lewis had predicted though probably not in the way he had expected—with the Devil at the top and Wormwood struggling to survive. The leading role of *Screwtape* was given to the great actor, Sir Donald Wolfit; the title role to the young and brilliant actor Hywel Bennett. At first Sir Donald was congenial. "I'll fit in," he said to Forsyth. "People say I'm trouble, dear boy. Not true." But he was. As soon as the contract was signed, he dominated the director, the stage, and the cast, and re-wrote passages and would accept little direction. He went out and ordered his own costume (a monstrous affair) and then—to quote the playwright—"played devilishly well at the expense of everyone and the play." When it got to Golders Green's old Hippodrome there were full houses. But the producers were unable to get a London theater to accept the production with Wolfit, and were advised to close the play and cast another *Screwtape.*

Dear Wormwood expired in Hull. The playwright was a casualty to nervous exhaustion and the experience of facing up to Wolfit. Once, in Oxford, in a dressing-room encounter when Forsyth was trying to make peace with Wolfit and induce him to rehearse, Wolfit snapped, "Do you realize, Mister Forsyth, that you are talking to the greatest actor the British stage has seen in the last 40 years?"

Since then, though the playwright lost heart and has done nothing about getting a professional production, the Dramatic Publishing Company proceeded to publish the play and it is now enjoying some success with amateur and stock companies in the United States under the title of *Screwtape!*

Perhaps the devil resented being up-staged by Wormwood, even in the title. "And Lewis would have smiled," says Forsyth, "he would see the *humor* of the situation."

In Canada, thirty miles north of Winnipeg, is St. John's Boys' School. It is tough. Believing there comes a time when one swat is worth a thousand words, boys are spanked unashamedly. Homework not done? Whack, Whack. Result: homework done. After the first month of school, each autumn, about a dozen new boys drop out. To allow for this, overenrollment is accepted. The annual drop-out rate is about 20 percent. The reasons often involve too much work in class, in choir practices, in the kitchen (the boys wash up), in the barn (the boys run a farm); and because there is very little leisure, and no television. Instead of the usual team sports, there are snowshoe trips in winter, canoe trips in summer. The boys are average. The graduating class invariably achieves the required 60 percent for university entrance. There are more than 250 applicants for the vacancies available. The School was founded in 1957. By 1970 it had opened a sister school at Warburg, Alberta. The overall name is now St. John's Schools of the Prairies. For the teaching of French the Schools use *Hansard,* the official record of Parliamentary Debates in Ottawa, published daily in French and English. For the teaching of history the Schools use the works of Winston Churchill; for religion, the works of C.S. Lewis.

Lewis's greatest impact is emphatically in the United States. American enthusiasm is a wonderful thing. Consider the English writer who wrote a story for *The British Weekly.* It was published without causing the slightest ripple. Five months later editor Ellery Sedgewick published it in a 1934 spring issue of *The Atlantic Monthly.* The story sizzled from Boston to San Diego and back to New York and throughout the world, and prompted two films and one play. That is the short history of *Good-Bye Mr. Chips* by James Hilton. Or consider clergymen. My own parents were married in a small church in London, Ontario, by a Reverend Robert Norwood. Because he was an able preacher, Dr. Norwood was lured to a much larger church in Boston, then to a still larger one in Philadelphia, and finally to St. Bartholomew's in New York City. Colossal as it is, he filled it, and was much revered. Not from St. Bartholomew's, but from some Fifth Avenue church a deputation of deacons offered George MacDonald $20,000 a year after his lecture tour. Twenty thousand dollars in 1873! Is that enthusiasm or not? And what other nation would have offered it? MacDonald could have delivered the same lectures in local idiom in any country in Europe without cracking a peanut. Only America is moved to plead, "Please stay with us. Here is $20,000." And now this wondrous enthusiasm is fired by the tranquil might of C.S. Lewis. For nigh on twenty years American sales have led the world. And almost every one of his books is still in print today.

The most popular are the Narnian tales, which are selling over a million copies a year. The reason for this may be explained by Martha Seiple of Austin, Texas: "I discovered Lewis as a child when I came across a copy of *The Magician's Nephew* in the school bookmobile. I must have read that book fifteen times. I could not put my finger on the reason it left me with a feeling of exultation, or joy, or something very positive. Since then I've collected everything of his in print and have read some books several times."[33]

The New York Times reports that "there are C.S. Lewis societies in almost all fifty states and in about fifteen countries."[34] No. This is wrong. I asked the reporter, Israel Shenker, where he got this: apparently he was misinformed. A journalistic exaggeration! (This is one reason why Lewis never read newspapers.) There are Lewis groups in perhaps half a dozen states and in two or three other countries. And it is quite true that in North America four periodicals devoted to Lewis have sprung up quite independently from each other, and are all flourishing—The *Bulletin* of The New York C.S. Lewis Society (1969); The *Chronicle* of The Portland C.S. Lewis Society (1972); The *Lamp-Post* of The Southern California C.S. Lewis Society (1974); and *The Canadian C.S. Lewis Journal* (1979).

Professor Thomas Howard says Lewis understood the improbability of awakening stultified modern imagination to ancient eternal blisses and realities.[35] Yes, but he has done it! And surely to a degree he would hardly have believed possible. For it is estimated that the total sales of his books throughout the world number about fifty million copies.[36]

One wonders what these staggering figures would have meant to Lewis himself? Well, he did see it coming. And here we have the impression of a close observer, Leonard Blake:

> Engaged and later married to Maureen Moore, I was in and out of the Kilns for years. I went to church with Lewis. I was with him at meals and in the garden and occasionally in his study. All that time from 1938 on, before and after he made those broadcasts and wrote those books that made him a world figure, I was about. He would join in family conversation, however silly or mundane, usually with some illuminating remark, or at least something interesting. He was always interested and interesting. But you would never dream that in his head those talks and books were being evolved. I could scarcely believe that the man passing me the jam at tea or kneeling beside me at church, had achieved international renown. Few writers can have shown greater indifference to the impact his works were making on the world ar large.[37]

This is one of several drawings in a current German issue of Lewis's *The Screwtape Letters, Dienstanweisung für einen Unterteufel,* which means "service instructions for an under-devil." Presumably, these are the smart, skeptical, vaguely pacifist people whose "subtle play of looks and tones and laughs," Screwtape is so pleased to write about in Letter X. (Drawing by H.E. Köhler; used with permission of the publishers, Verlag Herder, Freiburg, Germany.)

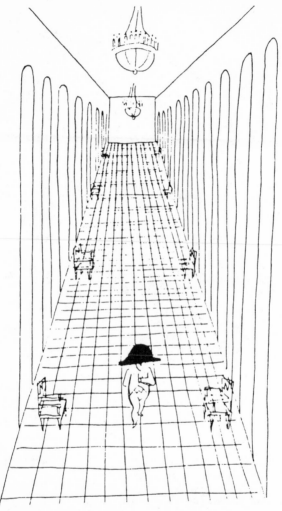

Lewis readers will immediately identify the above scene from *Die Grosse Scheidung,* a German edition of *The Great Divorce* by C.S. Lewis. The little Frenchman walking up and down, his mind repeating, "It was Ney's fault . . . it was . . . if only . . . ."—(Used with permission of the publishers, Johannes Verlag, Einsiedeln.)

— 19 —

Oxford Loses a Genius

Stephen Schofield

Taking an overall look at Lewis's career, perhaps the most astonishing fact is that during his time at Oxford he was never offered a professor's chair. And in all the history of the University it is doubtful if such a thing has ever happened before. For here we have the fact that Lewis, his "genius instantly recognized,"[1] denied a created chair, three times passed over for vacant professorships, and finally departing to a chair created especially for him at Cambridge. Why did it happen? That is the question. The cumulative force against Lewis is as old as Magdalen Tower, and about as difficult to budge. To relate why he was held down by Oxford authorities is not easy. It may be helpful to take a brief look at other speakers and writers, and their media, who were trying to reach the British public.

A contemporary of Lewis's, for example, was Vernon Bartlett, a radio commentator much like America's Walter Lippmann or Edward R. Murrow. Bartlett had been Paris correspondent for *The Daily Herald,* and for a time he broadcast on foreign affairs for the British Broadcasting Corporation. At this time, during the thirties when America had several such commentators on the air, Bartlett was the only one in Britain. The BBC took Bartlett off the air—not for anything he had said—but because he had too large a following. That was the reason—too large a following.[2]

Consider printing. The essential point about the whole business of printing—and it certainly concerns Lewis—is that in America, from the start, the printer came hard on the heels of the post office and grew up with the pony express. He printed news. And there was no one to stop him. In England, on the other hand—as Lewis himself relates—as soon as printing was invented, the government wanted to control what was printed; this control was exerted chiefly by the Stationers Company, incorporated by Royal Charter.[3] This control continued even into this century. Because they were afraid of newspapers, successive governments levied such heavy taxes that it was nearly impossible for a newspaper to be viable. They had to be subsidized by rich men. Even today British newspapermen are in a weak position. They know they are less respected than Americans. "There is no British equivalent to the American journalist-pundit—Reston, Lippmann, or the Alsops. American newspapers helped to create their democracy, spreading news from coast to coast—in a country without traditional social networks, journalism was crucial. But in Britain, the secretive ruling classes had no love of journalism, and it began as an eavesdropping profession, where even parliamentary reports had to be smuggled out. In spite of such eminent journalists as Churchill, Milner or Dickens, journalism has never quite recovered from this back-door complex."[4]

Even when *Pilgrim's Regress* was published in 1933 the British people had no daily newspaper. That is to say the masses had not been reached by the daily press. Lord Northcliffe, the great journalist and founder of the *Daily Mail,* had never reached them. The conditions that caused strikes, the Bryant and May match girls' strike, for instance—young girls working for nine shillings a week in conditions that condemned many to early death—the kind of news on which American journalism had been flourishing for years, was not reflected in Northcliffe's *Daily Mail.* He reached lower on the British social scale than any newspaper owner ever had. But he did not try to reach the masses. They had not enough money to spend to merit a market for advertisers.

The millions at the base of the British social pyramid had to wait until 1934 when a rugged character by the name of Harry Bartholomew began to attract them with the *Daily Mirror.* It was dying when he took over. He raised its circulation from 700,000 to 4,350,000—the largest in the world. Because nearly all its readers had had to leave school at the age of fourteen, this could only be achieved by sledgehammer tactics and brief sentences requiring a minimum of knowledge and a minimum of concentration. Thus, when Franklin Roosevelt had been president of the US for about a year, were the British masses first reached by daily journalism.[5]

Radio listeners had to wait longer. Sir John Reith, director-general of the BBC, dismissed as craven any suggestion that the BBC should concern itself with mass tastes. A journalist acquaintance of mine, radio columnist Collie Knox, needled Reith about this for years, with some effect. But Reith knew who had given him his job, and if he wanted to hold it and become Lord Reith, as he did at the end of his tenure, he knew whose tastes he had better cater to, and he did it.

The BBC did not offer Lewis the microphone in any hope that he might reach the masses. The book which prompted the BBC to invite Lewis was *The Problem of Pain,* an abstruse little volume, certainly to me. Surprisingly to Lewis and to the BBC, Lewis broke through to hundreds of thousands. The talks were published. Sales soared. Lewis became a household word. And thus his predicament began. And it should be clear that the chief reason why Lewis was hated in Oxford was on account of his popularity outside Oxford.[6]

Now, the really odd thing in the eyes of a Canadian journalist is this. The colleges of Oxford defy description. The gardens and libraries and dining halls, the woodwork and windows of chapels that leave one dumb, gaping in awe—what is it all about, really? Holman Hunt's painting, "The Light of the World," in Keble College Chapel—who was Keble? A clergyman. Pusey House—who was Pusey? Another clergyman. Whose statue is at the top of Magdalen Tower? Mary Magdalen's of course. Jesus College. Christ Church College. The whole University is based on religion. And it was for broadcasting religion—not law or medicine or science—that Lewis was hated and ostracized[7] in Oxford. It is more than odd. It is staggering.

Lewis was not hated by students. He was hated by senior Oxonians in key positions.[8] My own experience with these gentlemen is slight. I have met only one. He was a titled head of a college and had written one or two books about Homer; and he was a member of the professors' appointments committee. When he emerged from his office to speak to me in the corridor, he made it clear that he had more important things to do than to spend precious minutes with a journalist. This behavior was the exact opposite of Lewis's. My only other experience with official Oxford was with another college to whom I had addressed a brief query. They dealt with this in the easiest possible manner. They never answered it. Again, the exact opposite of Lewis. He was a model of *politesse*. So was his brother. I have about a dozen letters from him too. As prompt, polite letter writers I would say there was no choice between the brothers.

Writing to his brother in 1931, C.S. Lewis already alludes to the long tedious hours of tutorials.[9] "Of course," a Lewis pupil tells me, "he should not have been a tutor for so long. He clearly should have been a professor at the age of thirty-five."[10] Aged thirty-five! Well, he was fifty-three when he was passed over for the third time, in 1951, for a professorship of poetry. The foremost campaigner on this occasion was Dr. Enid Starkie.[11] She was a power in Oxford politics. She asked C. Day Lewis, a poet, to stand; and for weeks she worked to induce MAs to nominate him. Her flair for publicity attracted wide interest. C. Day Lewis won.[12]

The Daily Telegraph reported that Lewis "was obviously disappointed not to have been offered a chair by his own university; in particular, he was sad to be defeated by only a few votes [nineteen] for the professorship of poetry."

An American pupil, George Bailey,[13] says, "It is almost impossible to exaggerate Lewis's prestige in post-war Oxford. His preeminence in the field of English letters was unique. There was [Nevill] Coghill. There was Lord David Cecil. There were Wrenn, and C.T. Onions. But they were all, however impressive in themselves, only foothills in the shadow of the towering grandeur of Lewis."[14] One of the gentlemen Bailey mentions tells me that Lewis was by far the greatest man in Oxford during all his time there. These views may be exaggerated, though probably not much.

The performance of vengeance by educated Oxonians, in the eyes of a Canadian journalist, is extraordinarily interesting. Steeped in the finest work ever written in English, Latin and Greek—one might think their minds would be so civil as to be glad to award so illustrious a don as Lewis. They were not.

Perhaps a more important point is why they did it. I asked a Lewis pupil this question. He answered with some vehemence in one word: Jealousy! To some extent he is probably right. But apart from the usual envy and jealousy, another factor intervened. An Oxford don can speak and write for the intelligentsia, and perhaps a little below it. But he imperils his career if he explains the treasures of English literature in the idiom of the masses. Flinging pearls to the multitude is not the thing to do.[15] (The Apostles did it,[16] but they were not Oxford dons.) Lewis did not quite reach readers of the *Daily Mirror*. He came close enough to ruffle the feathers of some pretty cocky birds along the High, as Oxford's main thoroughfare is called. Major W.H. Lewis told me: "Jack [C.S. Lewis] was by no means universally popular here. There were people in Oxford, important and self-important, who were unknown to the outside world, and not a few of whom bitterly resented the fact that Jack had a following to whom his tenure of a Fellowship at Oxford was a minor detail in his career. *Hinc illae lacrimae.*"[17]

Lewis himself remarks that in every institution there is something which sooner or later works against the very purpose for which it came into existence.[18] When he says every institution he means every institution. One may not expect such a thing in Oxford. But apparently he is right. For there it is.

In post-war years there was much ill feeling toward Lewis. Christopher Derrick, back from the war to Magdalen College, says that "the president, Sir Henry Tizard, gave a sherry party for us returned heroes. In the course of it, he asked me what I was going to read.

" 'English.'

" 'Oh, so you'll be studying under the *great* C.S. Lewis. Oh, what an advantage. Oh, what an inestimable privilege.' He went on and on, in terms of the heaviest, most malevolent irony.

"Tizard was very much one of the 'top people,' e.g. in his wartime work with Churchill, etc. In his view, and that of many at Oxford, anyone who addressed 'bottom people' and got a hearing among them was guilty of the most vulgar demagoguery, this being all the more vulgar if one spoke about *religion* (of all things!) and, worse still, of religion as seen in orthodox terms. When I told Lewis that my eldest son had got a Demyship (scholarship) at Magdalen, he replied, 'What has the poor boy done, that you should send him alone and unarmed into that nest of crooks and atheists.' "[19]

Lewis's pupil George Bailey remarks that though there was constant discussion of Lewis's scholarly works, he never heard anyone, including the college chaplain, discuss his religious works at Oxford.[20] Talks by Lewis, so clear and short![21] The universe explained in a few pages! So advantageous to any chaplain! One might wonder why the Magdalen Chaplain would not be handing out copies right and left, and congratulating Lewis with all the ardor he could muster? Why not? My guess is the same old thing. Churches were largely empty. "The church has not lost the working class," says Dean Stuart Barton Babbage, "the working class was never in it. Since the days of the Industrial Revolution, the church's impact on the working class has been minimal."[22] Along comes Lewis broadcasting religion throughout Britain. Bishops must have winced at the impact. Overt support of Lewis could endanger a chaplain's career. So he kept his mouth shut. And who can blame him?

Even as a young man—in 1929—Lewis encountered hostility of the old regime in his own college. "At Magdalen he stood some nasty bullying from the College President for urging the recruitment of students by merit rather than social class. Lewis wanted to get away from the concept of a college as a finishing school for aristocratic youth."[23]

Concerning the aristrocracy, the last of the great aristocrats, a certain Lord X, served for a time as chancellor of Oxford University; and also, briefly, as acting prime minister. Only by a hair did he miss becoming prime minister. And how he wanted it! In England he had four grandiose residences. Once he dismissed a housemaid for allowing a footman to spend the night with her, although Lord X himself, for eight years, carried on an impassioned affair with a stunningly beautiful redhead who was married to a drunkard. When the drunkard died, Lord X unexpectedly ignored the widow, to whom he had given a diamond ring, and married a rich American, also very beautiful. Well, I happened to be writing an article about Lord X.[24] And because Major W.H. Lewis—always helpful!—was a contemporary of his, I asked him about this man. Major Lewis replied strongly by concluding, "In the Army feeling was strong against him . . . the damned Oxonian prig." Damned Oxonian prig! I was surprised to hear that from him.

Other events suggest a similar view. When the parcel of 225 C.S. Lewis letters to Greeves arrived from Ireland, addressed to Major Lewis, together with a letter from Greeves's next-of-kin, saying that Greeves had bequeathed them to the University of Oxford Library (the Bodleian), and, not knowing its address, asking Major Lewis to send them there, he did nothing of the kind. He sent them to the C.S. Lewis Collection, subsequently expanded and renamed the Wade Collection at Wheaton College, Illinois. Again when Major Lewis had a literary treasure of his own, a carefully kept diary of something in the region of a million words, he bequeathed it to Wheaton College. There it is.[25] And no copy is in Oxford.

Again Major Lewis helped me, this time in finding a letter which sheds more light on the same point. I was looking for a C.S. Lewis letter in which he says official Oxford consists of a lot of lazy old men, useful for nothing.[26] He says more than that. It is almost too strong to quote. What appears is an entrenched oligarchy, part of what might be termed a hierarchical horse that has trotted through England for centuries. The reins had been in well-bred hands for so many years. That was the crux. The key to England is the desire that knowledge and power should be sustained at the top. What really riled these Oxonians was that when Lewis acquired a vast following they saw power slipping through their fingers which loved to hold the reins. Lewis was gaining power; they were losing it. That riled them.

When Lewis had actually left Oxford, someone said mournfully, "They would have left less of a void if they had taken the Martyrs' Memorial."[27]

Well, of those who did hold him down, in their favor is evidence of penitence—later. In 1957, more than two years after Lewis had accepted the specially created Professorship of Medieval and Renaissance Literature at Cambridge, Oxford offered him, not a specially created chair, but a professorship caused by a vacancy. He declined.

"At Cambridge," Major Warren Lewis told me, "Jack felt almost at once in his proper element, both socially and professionally. And indeed I think he regretted that he had not in 1917 decided on Cambridge in preference to Oxford."[28]

About Cambridge, the Rev. Canon Adam Fox is also illuminating. Canon Fox was Chaplain at Magdalen College and also an Inkling with Lewis for several years. After visiting Lewis at Cambridge, Canon Fox later told me, "Cambridge suited Lewis much better than Oxford. We had lunch in the common room. (Magdalene College, Cambridge). Several people were there. Lewis took his share in the conversation. But he didn't take more than his share. He was very careful about that. He often spoke a great deal when he was engaged in discussion of interest to him, something he knew about. But he was not the sort of person who would collar conversation at all. And he was more happy than at Oxford. He hardly had tutorials at Cambridge—perhaps one or two, a few exceptional people. Everyone thought he was more happy at Cambridge."[29]

Lewis himself remarks that the atmosphere at Cambridge is far more kindly and gentle than Oxford.[30] Again he says Magdalene is much nicer to stay at than Magdalen.[31]

It is perhaps noteworthy—especially in America—that until 1948 another remnant of the old regime still prevailed in Oxford and Cambridge. University *graduates* had two votes. In national elections university graduates were represented, quite separately, by about a dozen Members of Parliament. This gave each graduate two votes: one where he lived, say, in London; and another vote in the constituency of his old university, Oxford, Cambridge, Edinburgh, and so forth.

Also in force was another two-vote arrangement. Business owners had two votes! One as a citizen, one as a business owner.[32] If a man lived, say, in Windsor, he would have one vote there, and if he owned a business in London, he would have another vote in that London consituency. All this power emanating from top people is really part of the hierarchical horse that managed to get a kick in at Lewis.

The same year these voting laws were abolished, 1948, another kick struck Lewis from a different angle. He wrote an article entitled, "The Humanitarian Theory of Punishment." In this he claims that governments are comprised of fallen men and are therefore neither very wise nor very good, usually unbelievers, and sometimes very wicked. In short, the article is favorable to prisoners at the bottom and unfavorable to the powers that be at the top. And the point that makes it pertinent to this chapter is that Lewis, then at the peak of his fame and surely an attractive name to an editor, could not get the article printed in England. And that, as he remarks at the end, is why he sent it to an Australian quarterly.[33]

Lionel Adey says, "Lewis was denied promotion for having demeaned himself" by becoming a popular broadcaster of religion rather than confining himself to literary scholarship.[34] Demean himself! He did nothing of the kind. If a man discovers something infinitely important, should he confine it to a coterie, or broadcast it as widely as possible? Along with Bunyan and Booth and others, Lewis ennobled himself. Make no mistake about that.

The overall point remains. That he came to Oxford was a great stroke of luck for the University. Such astonishing brilliance might as likely have appeared at the Sorbonne, or Yale or Harvard. He came to Oxford. Oxford recognized his genius, did nothing about it, and lost him. He left and would not return.

GEORGE MACDONALD

— 20 —

The Master: George MacDonald

Stephen Schofield

"I have never," says Lewis, "concealed the fact that I regarded George MacDonald as my master. Indeed I fancy I have never written a book in which I did not quote from him. But it has not seemed to me that those who have received my books kindly take sufficient notice of the affiliation. Honesty drives me to emphasise it. It must be more than 30 years ago I bought—almost unwillingly, for I had looked at the volume on that bookstall and rejected it on a dozen previous occasions—a copy of *Phantastes*.[1] A few hours later I knew I had crossed a great frontier."[2] *Phantastes,* a fairy story, first caused a trickle from a heavenly spring which finally broke Lewis's atheism and brought his work to millions. It is almost certain that without MacDonald Lewis would be known only to highbrow readers. This chapter is a brief look at MacDonald.[3]

In the introduction of a current edition of *Phantastes,* it is said that MacDonald enjoyed a horsie boyhood, a rare and beautiful relationship with his father, a happy marriage, and a career crowded with success. This is true, but misleading. He also suffered much failure and poverty and illness. He often prayed against anger, "Keep me from wrath; let it never seem so right." One brother, one sister, and four of his own children, died of tuberculosis. And in old age he lost his wife, and his voice.

He married on the strength of a job as minister of a church in Arundel. Not for long. Within three years he was sacked for preaching that heathens might *not* be everlastingly damned. The dismissal was enforced by the deacons and senior members, not by the main body of the congregation who did not share their views. He was twenty-nine. His wife was expecting their second child. They moved to Manchester and for months the family lived from hand to mouth.[4]

For MacDonald writing was hard. He never became facile. But he was always, always writing, until the pencil trailed away from sheer fatigue. And by means of lecturing too, and occasional preaching, the family skimped along. His books gradually attracted a readership sufficiently large to induce American publishers to steal rights and publish in America.[5]

In London he astonished two Americans. One was the Reverend Samuel McComb, DD, of Harvard University, who said, "George MacDonald affords the most remarkable illustration known to me of the mysterious creative faculty of mind. In a dim, dingy church, in simple conversational English, he poured forth, apparently without effort, a stream of noble thoughts which woke responsive echoes in me. The audience he held in his hand. On the same day I heard Dr. Wescott in Westminster Abbey and also Mr. Spurgeon. Good as their sermons were, it was MacDonald's impression that yet remains. I have often wondered what was the secret of his fascination."[6]

"I shall never forget," says Dean Brown of the Yale University Divinity School, "the description given by a friend of mine of a service he attended in the city of London. The preacher was George MacDonald. For the lesson that morning he read the eleventh chapter of Hebrews, 'Faith is the substance of things hoped for, the evidence of things not seen . . . .' When the time came for the sermon, MacDonald said, 'You have all heard about these men of faith. I shall not try to tell you what faith is. There are professors who could tell you that much better than I could do it. I am here to help you believe.' There followed such a simple manifestation of the man's own faith in those unseen realities, as to beget faith in the minds of his hearers. His heart was in his work. And his delivery was effective because it rested back on the beauty of his own inner life."[7]

MacDonald's skill as a speaker and the sale of his books gave rise to a tour in America. Accompanied by his wife and one son, Greville, who records it, the tour was a great success. Mrs. MacDonald loved New England, not merely because she saw her husband overwhelmed by enthusiastic people, rather because they had suffered so much failure and hardship, and now at last it seemed he was recognized. To the children at home she wrote from Boston, "The people are so glad to see Papa! I can't tell you how happy it seems to make some people to look at him. There were 2,850 ticket-holders. And such a hall! With two balconies all around it, to see those eager faces listening almost breathlessly, was a sight I shan't forget." Through New Jersey, Pennsylvania, Ohio and Illinois, often in small towns, up to Chicago, Toronto and Montreal, and back to Boston. "See here, Mr. MacDonald! Why didn't you *say* you could do this sort of thing? We'd have got $300 a lecture for you!"

When he spoke in Ann Arbor on a Sunday churches were closed so that everyone could hear him. One man pleaded to hear more, to work for him, to pay for passage and act as a servant in England. In Boston, in addition to lecture fees, he was given an outright gift of $1,500. MacDonald became friendly with Samuel Clemens (Mark Twain) who told him that he used an agent to sell his work abroad, and that every author ought to be connected to a robber of this kind.

Towards the end of the tour he spoke in New York, "Let there be no lies between us. The thinking of honest men on both sides of the Atlantic are just like each other. I trust that we in England and you in America, who have the same blood, the same language, the same literature, will only be friends. For the kindness I have received in America I am very grateful. Your big hearts, huge in hospitality and welcome, have been very tender to me and mine." After his last lecture in New York a deputation of deacons from a Fifth Avenue church offered him an annual salary of $20,000 to become pastor. He declined.

Returning to England, the MacDonalds lived in London for some years; and for a time they rented an old farmhouse, Great Tangley Manor, at Wonersh, Surrey. They all enjoyed this and MacDonald himself rejoiced in the fact that it was built in 1582 when Shakespeare was a boy. Wonersh is near my home. I went over to see the house. The property is now enhanced by a water garden, a moat, and a swimming pool. But the Tudor style of the house, oak-beamed within and without, the paneled walls and leaded windows and deep fireplaces, are exactly as when MacDonald lived in it, and long before that. Upstairs in the master bedroom the four-poster canopy bed where Mr. and Mrs. MacDonald slept is as solid as ever—I felt it—and it is still used by the present owners.

MacDonald kept a horse in Surrey, as indeed he did in London, and rode whenever possible, even when visiting his sister in Scotland. His father had insisted on his learning to ride bareback before using a saddle. In Surrey, the horse once placed a forehoof on Greville's shoulder as a gesture of affection. That MacDonald loved animals, especially horses, and believed that such good beings as animals would continue after death, is evident in his novels. After a few warm pages on horses, for instance, is this: "Do you think God would invent such a delight for his children as the society and love of animals, and then let death part them forever? I don't."[8]

Alas, he did not heed the advice of Mark Twain to use an agent who knew how to rap on desks and pit one publisher against another. Such aggressiveness was alien to MacDonald, who had the gentleness of a child. He did not squeeze publishers. They squeezed him. Whipping himself to work like a machine every day, by the time he was fifty he had written twenty-three books; and his assets amounted to eight pounds in the bank and five pounds in his pocket, as he casually mentions in a letter to his wife. Lewis says MacDonald's poverty was very great. This may be an exaggeration, but not much. At times the family was on the brink of starvation, though the sales of his books, including robbed editions, were not far behind those of Dickens and Thackeray.

To alleviate financial difficulties, Mrs. MacDonald set the family to work as a theatrical troupe, producing Shakespearean and other plays, chiefly "A Pilgrim's Progress." This dismayed all relations and many friends because acting was then considered a disreputable profession. The MacDonalds persevered and made money. They had to. MacDonald himself was often ill from bronchial trouble, as he had been even in America; and now his lungs became diseased and the family was compelled to spend winters in Italy. They all pitched in and produced. MacDonald earned quite a name for himself as Mr. Greatheart in "A Pilgrim's Progress." His wife became adept at stagecraft, making the most of simple props; and only daughter, Lila, was a born actress of professional caliber. Local newspapers gave ample space to their efforts. Of course such a family producing presentable drama was in itself news. The motive was to make enough money to support the family during the winter in Italy. And that, summer after summer, for years, is what they did.

Much happened in Italy. MacDonald flourished. The heat was a tonic. Sitting by a window overlooking the sea and a grove of orange trees, he turned out page after page. Mrs. MacDonald played an old organ in the rented house. Friends and relations from England were annoyed by the MacDonalds' inviting Italian children from the town to attend concerts and bonfire parties that they joyfully participated in. Relations were more annoyed by a MacDonald concert—open to anyone and by payment only—all proceeds going to the new Catholic church in the town. Of course the local priest was elated and embraced MacDonald whenever they met on the street. Mrs. MacDonald also played the organ in the town church and trained the choir. MacDonald gave courses in Shakespeare and Dante. The family adopted two little girls and their consumptive mother who was penniless and abandoned by her French husband. Two MacDonald daughters undertook to educate the girls, and did so. At Christmastime, armed with lanterns and sheets of music, the family visited local invalids and sang carols for them. Such was the family.

Towards the end of his life MacDonald wrote to his son, "Next December I shall be seventy. I am glad at the thought of being so near Home now."[9] And surely, though he lived to be eighty-one, that is where he went. Overall, MacDonald appears to have been a deeply happy man and a prodigious worker. Lewis says MacDonald's peace of mind came not from building for the future but from living in what he called the sacred present.[10] He was careful not to let himself compete with others: "No ambition to be a motive, no wish to surpass another to be allowed a moment's respite from death."[11] Lewis calls this "killing the nerve."

"MacDonald's central belief was in the gradual transformation of the lower self into the higher self by the willing of the death of the lower self (self-abnegation), but the transforming power was the presence of Christ within, and his emphasis on subjective experience and guidance by the Divine spirit was not at the expense of the objective reality of God. Man is subsumed in that reality. MacDonald also was a universalist believing that all humanity would eventually be saved since God was too loving a Father to leave one straying sheep."[12] Another salient trait of MacDonald's was his view of a child. To him, childhood was not something to grow out of. It was a state of mind to aspire to. How far he achieved this may be indicated by Lewis's first impression of *Phantastes*. Lewis says the whole book has about it a cool morning innocence. This may be the child in MacDonald. And perhaps it was chiefly this childlike quality that broke through to Lewis and finally brought him to you and me.

— 21 —

Letters to an Editor

Stephen Schofield

Some of the chapters in this book have been used in
The Canadian C.S. Lewis Journal. *The following letters give*
readers' personal reactions to those articles. Some of the
letters reveal further insights into the life of C.S. Lewis.

Exhilaration

The account by Kenneth Tynan about testing Lewis's extraordinary memory, reminds me of a somewhat similar event.

I came up to Magdalen College to read English language and literature and to work with Lewis in 1954. I soon learned that he had been elected to a chair at Cambridge and never had tutorials with him.

The students at Magdalen who were reading English belonged to a club called the Florio Society, named for John Florio, a member of the College and a literary figure of Elizabethan England. The only activity of the Society I remember was a dinner given in the oldest part of the College as a farewell for Lewis. I suppose the date was in November, 1954.

We were seated at a long table with C.S. Lewis at one end and J.A.W. Bennett at the other. Bennett, who was then a colleague of Lewis at Magdalen for many years, followed him in the Cambridge chair, from which he has since retired. After dinner, the port circulated and conversation became expansive. Lewis was asked about his current writing and grumbled a bit about having found that he was concluding many of his paragraphs with iambic pentameter.

Seated near him was an American Rhodes scholar, Richard Selig, a poet of energetic mind and considerable spirit. He responded in pressing manner to the remark.

Selig asked, "If you *will* end your paragraphs in iambic pentameter, why do you grumble about it, sir?"

Lewis replied, "As usual, Selig, you missed the point. The difficulty is that I remember everything I've ever read and bits pop up uninvited."

"Surely not *everything* you've ever read, Mr. Lewis?"

"Yes everything, Selig, even the most boring texts."

By now the end of the table was silent and waiting to see if Selig would drop the matter; but he backed off from very little.

Selig got to his feet and went to the College library, which was open late in term, and took out a volume of the long and little-read poem. He returned and opened the volume. He read a few lines.

"Stop!" said Lewis who lifted his eyes toward the ceiling and began to recite the poem in his rich and modulated public voice. He stopped after ten lines or so and looked at Selig, now very silent. Conversation was slow to resume at that end of the table.

I have told that story often. The parallels with Tynan's account are interesting. A final point is this. Lewis would cringe at the developing level of hagiographical material about him. He had sharp edges to his nature and could be severe, especially with slackers or the self-indulgent. He did not like soft-minded criticism of his work either. I urge you not to try to sanctify him in your Journal. He would have hated that and despised you for falsifying with uncritical goodwill: the exact characteristic that fueled his mildly anti-American and anti-Canadian sentiments.

> (Dean) John Leyerle
> Professor of English
> School of Graduate Studies
> University of Toronto

In your interview with Malcolm Muggeridge, he says that there was something "inscrutable" about Lewis and had something to do with Lewis's attitude toward women.[1] Mr. Schofield, agreeing, refers to the story that Lewis ran away and hid when a woman was in college. But this rather silly story has been answered by Lewis himself, pointing out that he had numerous female pupils and adding that if he ever secluded

himself from a woman it was not because she was female but because
she was a bore. There is of course a difference.

Mr. Schofield further supports the idea of prejudice in commenting:
"But the prejudice slips out sometimes. He says (In *A
Preface to Paradise Lost*) Eve is the mother of all corrupting
female novelists. Why pick on females? There are quite as
many corrupting male novelists, possibly more. Again
(*Letters* July 9, 1927) he approves of the rule of limiting the
number of women at Oxford. And he says somewhere
(*Letters* February 3, 1927) that lecturing to women is apt to
be dangerous, or words to that effect."
This certainly does look like prejudice. But let us look at the remarks in
context.

In *A Preface to Paradise Lost* Lewis is not of course talking about
the Old Testament story of the fall but of Milton's. And it is *Milton,* not
Lewis, who shows Eve to be *far* more corrupted than Adam: she is the
one with a megalomaniac lust for power, and she is guilty of murder in
intention. Adam, on the other hand, sins through uxuriousness,
excessive subjection to Eve; and, after his sin, he becomes worldly and
flippant. Lewis, then, characterises *Milton's* Adam and Eve, respectively,
as: "The father of all the bright epigrammic wasters and the mother of
all corrupting female novelists . . . ." The first is an accurate description
of a certain type of *man;* the second—and be it remembered that
Milton's Eve *has* corrupted Adam—of a certain type of *woman.* If Adam
had been a corrupter, he might have been likened to a corrupting male
novelist; since he wasn't, Lewis had no reason to mention the fact which
certainly had not escaped his attention, that male corrupting novelists
existed. Out of context, half the remark looks like prejudice: in context,
not at all.

What about Lewis's approval of limiting the number of women at
Oxford? The referenced letter is about a rather silly woman,
Mrs. Moreton, and about Congregation's limiting the number of
women. The part about Mrs. Moreton signifies nothing concerning
Lewis's attitude toward women—unless it could be shown that she was
not silly or that no woman could be silly. As to Congregation and the
rule limiting the number of women at Oxford, Lewis analyzes the
voting: the very old, he says, voted against women; the moderately old

voted for them; and the young men voted against them. What is interesting is his explanation of why they voted so: the very old were ignorant of women; the moderately old were romantic about women (as scholars); and the young men were realistic about women. Lewis himself of course was one of the young men—the post-Great-War generation—and I suspect that he had an accurate understanding of the opinions of his own generation. At all events, one might use the passage to prove that a whole generation was in error about women, but not to prove that Lewis had any prejudice that wasn't more or less shared by his generation. It of course was inferior in insight to our own.

The last item of the indictment is that Lewis thought that lecturing to women was dangerous. It cannot be borne out by the referenced letter.

Thus, finally, the three citations add up to precisely no proof at all that Lewis was prejudiced against women. Or for them, either, as of course some modern converts passionately are. It has always seemed to me, as it did to my wife, that Lewis was not only objective about women but showed in his portrayal of the Lady of *Perelandra* as well as that of the warrior-queen Orual a deep and sympathetic understanding of them.

Sheldon Vanauken
Lynchburg, Virginia

A Guest in the House

George Sayer's article provides the answers to some burning questions. I was deeply moved by the news that Lewis used a shaving stick called Erasmic. The fact that he wore Aertex cotton underwear fills me with awe. And the revelation that he used a chamber pot during the night will be extremely valuable for my spiritual life. Perhaps Professor Sayer was trying to write a parody on medieval hagiography?

Klaus Schaefer
Braunschweig
West Germany

An answer to that is this: "It is a peculiar trait in us all that makes us want to know everything about a great man. If we can find out how Johnson wanted his eggs, or whether Bismarck wanted his windows open or closed, we will. Data like this may or may not throw light on the man's contribution to the race—literature, politics, science, etc.—but it often seems to." Professor Thomas Howard, author of *The Achievement of C.S. Lewis,* in the Foreword of *C.S. Lewis: Speaker and Teacher,* edited by Carolyn Keefe (Zondervan).

—Editor

C.S. Lewis, the Teacher
Hurrah! The E.L. Edmonds article is tremendous, full of all sorts of good things.

(Professor) Clyde S. Kilby
Wheaton, Illinois

I read Professor Edmonds's account with great interest. Someone told me the other day that Lewis did not enjoy his tutorial teaching. Can this be true? He must have done it in such a stimulating and inspiring fashion, given, of course, he had a responsive pupil. But of course he was a modest man and may have felt that he never was as good a tutor as he should be. The evidence presented by Professor Edmonds shows that Lewis could be a wonderful tutor. But, indeed, conversation with him suggested that already. I found him consistently interesting to discuss literature with, as I found no one else in Oxford—such a blend of learning, thought and vivid sensibility. Our tastes were not always the same. For instance I could not share his enthusiasm for William Morris, nor he my love and veneration for Thomas Hardy; but these differences only added to the excitement of our talks—and anyway we loved many of the same authors, including Johnson, Jane Austen, Charles Lamb. We approached literature for what it was rather than for some "Oxford" standpoint.

(Lord) David Cecil
Cranborne, Dorset

Stunning Effect
Erik Routley's article "Stunning Effect" is as good as anything you've yet published. But I think that living in America may have clouded his memory of what it was like in Britain in June, 1940,

"pre-Eisenhower days," Dr. Routley calls them. We were *not* expecting to be "required to speak German by September." America did *not* win the war for us by her belated entry forced upon her by the Japanese, though obviously she helped to finish it sooner. Had Britain and her Dominions not stood fast in 1940—alone—America would not be free today. Nothing to do with Lewis. But I thought it right to set the record straight.

Peter Jackson
Croydon, Surrey

I have never heard of C.S. Lewis, and I suspect this is my intellectual loss. If you have time, please tell me something about him and why he apparently made such an impact.

John Bassett
Baton Broadcasting, Toronto

Though I am certainly not an authority, I will do my best, briefly.

At about the age of fourteen, because he so hated school—being so "different," unathletic and a constant "target" for the other boys—his father removed him from school and put him in the hands of a tutor, near Surrey. The tutor met young Lewis at the station. While being driven home, Lewis began chatting politely, remarking on "the unexpected wildness of the Surrey countryside . . . ."

"Stop," said the tutor, "what do you mean by 'wild' and what grounds have you for expecting it to be otherwise?"

Lewis could not well explain. "Do you not see, then," said the tutor, "that you had not right to an opinion on the point?" This recurred. And the steadfastness of the tutor did not alter one whit in all the years Lewis remained, very happily, with him. And this trait of accuracy, dead accuracy as far as possible, and first knowing what he was trying to be accurate about, remained with him all his life, such that today, when the New York C.S. Lewis Society asks new members a customary question, "What was Lewis's most pronounced characteristic?" most of them answer, "Clarity."

He was careful not to allow himself to be distracted by events of his own era. He told me himself that he hardly read any contemporary literature: and by this I would say he meant anything written during the last 150 years. He considered this era no more or less important than Victorian or Shakespearean times, and others long before that. He read them all and considered them all. Even a cursory glance at some of his work reveals an astonishing breadth of thoroughly assimilated ancient literature. He believed a book merits study only if it has been tested "against the great body of thought down the ages." Lewis claimed that all periods, on close inspection, turn out to be full of alarms and crises; that human life has always been lived on the edge of a precipice; and that a scholar who has lived in many eras is in some degree immune from the torrent of trash that pours from the press and radio of his own era.

Like a razor, he cuts through verbosity, pretence, the ever-so-little lie, and all desire to present himself in favor. Lewis wrote, "Priests are wicked men like the rest of us."

Others would think, "Oh, I must not put it that bluntly; it might antagonize the Church or my employers. Will it look well for me or my business?" The motive on which North America so largely revolves, never entered his mind. His test was simply, "If it is right, then write it."

> Editor
> Dunsford, Surrey

The Butcher

Alan Rook tries to prove the *coldness* of C.S. Lewis. If he were such a man how could he have written so patiently and with such compassion to the American lady (*Letters to an American Lady*, edited by Clyde Kilby) who persisted in correspondence for thirteen years? He sent her a regular allowance to supplement her income, and corresponded faithfully with her up to the time of his death. Many people I know who knew Lewis or visited him speak of his warmth and courtesy to those in all walks of life.

> Dora Chaplin
> Staten Island, New York

Lewis's tutoring of me was very much like that described by Alan Rook: "I never felt any warmth—no real human contact—purely intellectual reasoning and fact—used as a foil—I'd nothing more to say—mentally depleted." He never really illuminated anything—of poetry, that is—he illuminated the meaning of words, the validity of arguments, and the changes of consciousness in writing, for me, but *not* the passion or the beauty of the poetry. All just as Major Rook says; and he was one of my generation there.

C.S. Lewis's greatest inspiration to me was not in any of these ways but in his teaching about the ambiguous meaning of words. As a professional myself, I value perhaps most *his* most professional work: his book, *Studies in Words.* This book is rarely mentioned because it is technical. Before George Orwell, Lewis was warning me of "double talk" —of the way the subtle changes in the meanings of words must be watched by those trained to see them—not to moralize but to clarify. He instilled in me the belief that it was the great mission of any educator to make others aware of how words could be, instead of communicators, the great "blurrers" of real communication.

I must add that the real eye-opener to me at Oxford was not anything Lewis said but Nevill Coghill's lectures in Exeter College on 'The Growth of Human Consciousness from Chaucer onwards' or some such title. I was never really the same again.

Norman Bradshaw
Titchfield, Hampshire

The article by Alan Rook raises an interesting point and could be important in our search for the character of Lewis.

Major Rook calls Lewis, if I do not misunderstand what he writes, cold and impersonal and austere. In contrast with what I remember of him, which was the character of a hearty, convivial and very outgoing person who, in every word he said, gave something of himself (and in every word he wrote in a private letter).

I am not in any sense contradicting Major Rook—which would be presumptuous; but Major Rook met Lewis as a professional, and I never did. I think it is likely that anybody who is near the top of the tree in any professional discipline appears austere to his equals; for they both value something—the same thing—so much that nothing but the most courteous precision in their attitude towards the subject will do. When equals see the same thing in a different way the disagreement can be profound and perhaps alarming, just as when they find they agree, the agreement produces a rare and precious warmth.

It is quite different when people meet on neutral ground. It is here, surely, that in Lewis one encountered the warm and ready laugh. I don't remember ever speaking to him—and I must make it clear that I didn't often have the chance to do so—without hearing that thoroughly rustic laugh. But then I simply wasn't in the business of English; indeed my own preoccupation was something he rather hated: church music.

No, I'm sure it's true that he never had any small talk. Neither, I think, did William Temple. Some people treat everything anybody says as important and so are incapable of keeping talk small. I met him once in a train—that blessed train that used to take half a day to run from Cambridge to Oxford. I was reading *Surprised by Joy* at the time. I put my head into a compartment he was alone in (British trains in those days were divided into little rooms seating eight people) and said, "I've got just to the bit where you say you hate being disturbed by casual strangers, but I hope all's well with you in Cambridge" (or something like that). With a roar of laughter Lewis said, "Well, Coriolanus did join Volsci; but no good came of it!" Incidentally, halfway through the journey Lewis came in and joined me in my compartment and we had an hour's conversation—the longest I ever did have with him. What I remember of that was precisely the small things I was capable of saying he always enlarged—which is just the point.

It would have been a very different matter had I been his pupil, and different again, in the same direction, had I been a brilliant one. Then, I think, the academic heat would have been on.

Erik Routley
Westminster Choir College
Princeton, New Jersey

I enjoyed reading the Major Rook interview. I have always been puzzled about the two sides of Lewis's personality that are invariably presented by various people who had met him: the kindly, jovial, humble man vs. the formidable, argumentative, strong personality. Certainly your interview seems to bring out the latter aspect very forcibly. Personally, I have met only one person who had been a student of Lewis's, and he, too, used the word formidable to describe him. However, after hearing Walter Hooper speak in Toronto at the showing of the film on Lewis's life, I got the impression—ambivalence again!—that one would have been comfortable and at ease on meeting him. So, I suppose, these opinions will go on. I try to keep up with new Lewis material. I have of course read Dr. Clyde Kilby's books; also Sheldon Vanauken's *A Severe Mercy.* I have been passionately fond of Lewis's writings for over twenty years and they have had a profound effect on my thinking.

Isobel Sabapathy
Islington, Ontario

Impressions of a Pupil

I was most interested in Norman Bradshaw's "Impressions of a Pupil." I remember the reference in Lewis's *English Literature in the Sixteenth Century,* his "learned pupil" who played a Tudor lyric on a recorder, thus bringing it "dancing to life." I agree with much of what Mr. Bradshaw says of the tutorials at Magdalen. Only once did I feel that I had failed to please with my essay. He was silent, or rather began to question me primly, and politely. It may have been different with the young men actually at Magdalen. He certainly never was "ungentlemanly." He would sometimes offer us tea and come to tea with us. But no question of alcohol with mere girls! I think perhaps he had a mistaken view of the effect of a girl's public school. For instance, in one of his books, *The Allegory of Love,* I think, he refers to a candidate or pupil from one. She evidently had expressed disgust at Spenser's description of a mother suckling a baby. He thought her attitude wrong and unnatural, as indeed it is. But in pre-war days girls' boarding schools sometimes wrongly made the pupils feel ashamed of normal bodily functions, such as perspiration. At mine, even bare legs were disapproved of! Fortunately, at my school, the headmistress was so extreme that most of us began to ridicule it all. So when I got to Oxford I used to quote another passage from Spenser in which the lady knight, Brirmart, is compared to a woman who, when she gives birth, is overjoyed, and so forgets the anxiety of her pregnancy. I do not know whether I quoted this to Lewis or not. But he can hardly have understood girls brought up under virtually Victorian, and so prudish discipline, especially over sex.

We did not have to agree with Lewis. He wanted to know the facts on which we based our opinions. If we were not waffling, he welcomed a fresh view. His method was Socratic. But he expected a bit more than, "Yes, Socrates!" We used to emerge from Magdalen still discussing the points raised.

Patricia (Thomson) Berry
London

Disappointment at Cambridge?

Professor Fryer's article, "Disappointment at Cambridge," was very good. But Lewis certainly seemed genuinely happy when I visited him at Cambridge and dined at the Magdalene high table. C.S. Lewis said later that it was a far gentler, kinder college than Magdalen, Oxford.

Sheldon Vanauken
Lynchburg, Virginia

I think much of Professor Fryer's article about Lewis is wrong. Lewis loathed administration and resigned as vice president after serving a single year. It is inconceivable that he should want to be president. He was certainly opposed to electing Tizard as president but that was because Tizard was a scientist.

Lewis went to Cambridge solely because the position of Professor offered him more leisure and more opportunity to write about the topics that interested him. The story that he was driven from Magdalen by left-wing colleagues is nonsense. Who are they? Me? Weldon.[2] McFarlane?[3] He may have spoken about some of us with exaggerated irritation but there was deep affection between us. He may have felt that the Faculty had treated him badly but I doubt even that.

A.J.P. Taylor

I agree with A.J.P. Taylor, and I find W.R. Fryer equally wrong in other respects which the former does not mention. The intellectual and moral tone at Cambridge *did* suit Lewis much better than that of Oxford. He felt much more at home there and frequently said so; and he did make new friends there, whom he valued highly.

Owen Barfield
South Darenth, Kent

Mr. Barfield was Lewis's closest friend for more than forty years. Lewis dedicated The Allegory of Love *to "Owen Barfield, wisest and best of my unofficial teachers."*

The Mystery

I certainly agree with you that there is a great deal of information about Lewis which has not been forthcoming. If you can explain why he did not like Americans, and why he married a dying American, I would be most grateful.

(Mrs.) Holly Wilkinson
Corona del Mar, California

Yes, Lewis's attitude slips out here and there. As a young man, near the end of the First World War, he mentions to his old friend Greeves what a pity it is that such an inspiring writer as Ralph Waldo Emerson is an American.[4] And some years later, during the thirties, he again confides to Greeves that one of his pupils is not really competent enough to write an essay on MacDonald, and apart from everything else, he adds, she is an American.[5] And the prejudice appears to have remained because even after the Second World War his American pupil George Bailey reports that "it was widely rumored that Lewis did not like Americans."[6]

Well, I was in England for a year during the thirties when anti-American feeling was fairly common. Apparently the aftermath of Prohibition and mounting crime, and such names as Capone,[7] Schultz and Dillinger, effused an unpleasant aura. After living in England for some years during the twenties and thirties, an American lady returned to Rhode Island and observed, "Was this America, my home? Even my father's Puritan drawl told me shyly he'd sold his yawl for a fabulous price to a constable's son, thought to be one of a criminal gang, such clever fellows with so much money, even the constable thought it funny, until one morning his son was found, floating dead on Long Island Sound. Was this my country? It seemed like heaven, to get back, dull and secure, to Devon, loyally hiding from Lady Jean and my English friends the horrors I'd seen."[8] For much the same reason and about the same time, Charles Lindbergh and his family fled from America to the comparative peace and order of England.[9] And during the same era

Thomas Wolfe writes of America, "Its lies, its horrible falseness, its murderous criminality."[10]

Often enough the kind of Americans who came over here were ill-mannered people who had made a lot of money quickly, and were apt to belittle the leisurely English way of doing things. An English lady gleefully told me of one such American, expatiating to the conductor of a London bus, "Why, we build buildings costing a million dollars, maybe two million, and get 'em up in six months."

The conductor became rather fed up with this; and when the bus passed by the Houses of Parliament and the American inquired, "What's that?" the conductor said, "I don't know. It wasn't there this morning."

Lewis mentions somewhere that George MacDonald was often praying against anger, "Keep me from wrath, let it never seem so right." One reason for this anger could well be that his stories appeared in America again and again; and not a penny paid to MacDonald.[11] American violation of international copyright law was a scandal.[12] We know Lewis read of these robberies recorded by MacDonald's son Greville.[13] And it can hardly have pleased Lewis, who well knew that MacDonald's "poverty was very great."[14]

Another factor that probably influenced Lewis is this. Lewis was a democrat because he believed in the fall of man and that no one, therefore, can be trusted with unchecked power over his fellows.[15] At the same time, he was a firm upholder of kings and queens, and rejoiced in the fact that Britain had maintained its monarchy. Lewis claims that the human spirits needs the nourishment a monarch provides; that people need someone to honor; otherwise they are apt to honor film stars and athletes, even gangsters, instead.[16] He does not pinpoint America; but the inference is plain.

And in *English Literature in the Sixteenth Century* Lewis says the discovery of America was one of the greatest disappointments in the history of Europe. There was, to be sure, adventure and glory in finding an immense, rich continent. But the real discoverer of America was Avarice. The finest minds in Europe were ashamed of Spanish and French greed in America.[17] Montaigne, for example, deeply regrets that such a rich discovery could not have fallen to the ancients, who might well have spread civility where the French have spread only corruption.[18] And the English, coming after the Spanish and French, and thus thwarted of much mineral wealth, had to be content with colonizing a land they considered suitable for troublesome people, an outlet for social sewage.[19] Lewis quotes all these writers who may well have influenced his view of Americans.

Overall, however, the rumor George Bailey reports in 1946 must have been false because, as Mr. Norman Bradshaw remarks, "After his war-time and post-war experience of food parcels and the invasion of Magdalen College from the States, this prejudice disappeared, as his 'Letters' clearly show."[20]

I now turn to his marriage. Why did he marry a dying American? Briefly, this is what happened.

Mrs. William Lindsay (Joy) Gresham[21] and her husband were card-carrying Communists until Lewis's books—in part, they claimed—brought about their belief in Christianity. She corresponded with Lewis and came to England and met him, first, in 1952. Her marriage disintegrated. She returned to the United States and divorced her husband who announced he was in love with another woman. He re-married. She, with her two sons, returned to England, in the opinion of one of Lewis's old friends, "to get Lewis."[22] For a time she acted as a sort of secretary to Lewis; and certainly he enjoyed her company, her quick wit, her sense of fun. The two Gresham boys attended school in Surrey. When, as they say in America, she let her hooks out, however gently, insinuating matrimonial intentions, Lewis shied away, even to the point of pretending to be out when she called. But when the British Government told her in effect that she would have to get out of the country by such and such a date, Lewis married her in a registry office on April 23, 1956. The sole reason he gave for this was to make it possible for her to stay in England; he thought this essential for the boys to remain at school, and for Joy's happiness. At this time he had no suspicion that she had cancer, though she may possible have had it: certain pains from which she was suffering were diagnosed as a form of rheumatism. The bedside marriage officiated by the Revd. Peter Bide on March 21, 1957, at the Churchill Hospital was so that she could *without scandal* be nursed at the Kilns.[23] The doctors said she had mere months to live, the nurses reckoned weeks. For Lewis, the confirmed bachelor who had so often throughout his life avoided women, the dominant motive was almost certainly, as Alan Rook remarks, compassion.[24] Joy was moved to the Kilns, and then the miracle occurred. She recovered and they had three precarious years together before she died. Although I have it from three unimpeachable sources that she was given to heated outbursts of bad temper which strained Lewis and shortened his life,[25] from all other reports the marriage was an uncommonly happy one. Lewis refers to it in several letters,[26] and in *A Grief Observed* he distinctly affirms the ecstasy of its consummation.[27] In all it appears that the marriage he undertook as a charitable duty turned out to be a crowning delight of his life.

The Fun of the Thing

I find nothing to disagree with Mr. Taylor violently about. It is, however, not true that Lewis did not like music. And Mr. Taylor is quite wrong about Dickens: what Lewis loved was not the story but the odd characters.

Owen Barfield
South Darenth, Kent

The Mystery

The discussion on Lewis and women with Malcolm Muggeridge was stimulating. But it illustrates the danger of generalizing about the attitude of any individual. We often assume that attitudes don't change, which, of course, is ridiculous. Lewis as a young bachelor and atheist may have been something of a misogynist. Or, if not a woman-hater, at least a masculine snob. But Christianity made a new man of him. And maturity ripened the man so that he could create a marvelously fresh and unique picture of Tinidril in *Perelandra,* the sensitive portrait of Jane Studdock in *That Hideous Strength,* the vibrant Lucy and Polly of the Narnian Chronicles, and the poignant glimpse of the heart of an ugly woman in Orual of *Till We Have Faces.* The place to find Lewis's views is where he wrote them. It is probably true that marriage opened his eyes to many things. But I doubt that the man who created the feminine characters I mentioned needed to make an about face after he married.

The annual C.S. Lewis Institute here was enjoyable. I would say Kay

Lindskoog was the star of the show. We are now planning another Institute. So interest in Lewis does not seem to be dying in the Pacific Northwest.

(Professor) Evan K. Gibson
Seattle Pacific University
Washington

I have just been reading Lewis pieces in Walter Hooper's collection of literary essays, and found the experience more refreshing than I had expected. I have been reading a good deal of Ronald Knox and the difference is striking. Knox has a very fine mind, perhaps as fine as Lewis's. But there is something about him I don't trust. I have a feeling that Knox is trying to make me believe something; and is quite prepared to do some subtle distortion or suppression of the facts in order to do it. The fact that it is usually something I believe does not alter my irritation at being propagandized. With Lewis I never have that feeling. You know he is a passionate believer; you know he wants you to share his beliefs; but you never suspect him of resorting to the least dishonesty to do it. On any given issue you feel strongly that Lewis believed every word he said; and that, if he had been shown to be wrong on any point, he would have abandoned that point. Lewis gets at the real man, or at least as near to the real man as anyone can. Honesty of the Lewis type is very rare, and absolutely priceless.

Charles Wrong
University of South Florida
Tampa, Florida

Oxford Loses a Genius
I enjoyed "Oxford Loses a Genius." O Academe! America's "Ivy" version is all too closely modelled on England's—right down to the infighting and discrimination.

S.S.W.
Boston

The value of what you have gathered into your article, "Oxford Loses a Genius," is indisputable. But your comments about the general background include points which strike me as uncharacteristic of how life really was at that time.

Oxford lost a genius in Lewis, and lost him by Oxford's own fault. Still, it is a fact that many dons view a fellowship (and Lewis's long tenure of the English fellowship at Magdalen must have been one of the most illustrious ever) as "a career in its own right." Many distinguished fellows never proceed further; yet no one thinks the worse of them for that.

Still: the fellows—were they the people "at the top," whose "well-bred hands" held the reins? It depends on what is meant by "the top." If it means the aristocracy: very few of them. I *knew* only one fellow connected with the peerage: the Reverend Canon Adam Fox, chaplain at Magdalen, who was said to be related to the Duchess of York, now the Queen Mother. And a better chap you could never hope to meet: a true Christian, a very decent scholar, a kind teacher and above all a *host* who kept open house, every night at 9:30, to all and sundry, to people from the great "public schools," to chaps like me from unheard-of grammar schools, to Slovaks, Japanese, Chinese, black people, to Christians, Muslims, Buddhists, unbelievers, Marxists and even Fascists: unfailingly welcoming, frank and "sharing." He was by no means an enemy of Lewis, and *theologically* rather more liberal than Lewis.

Also, I *heard,* though I did not know, Lord David Cecil, fellow of New College, and later professor; a nice enough chap surely, a very able expositor of his themes, an elegant writer, to whom C.S. Lewis once recommended (through me) a young Frenchman then anxious to write for his PhD about Disraeli's novels (and anyone more left-wing than this young Frenchman then was, you couldn't imagine).

Finally, I come to your comments on life in England during Lewis's years at Oxford. My rejoinders are two:

1. Were parliamentary seats for the Universities, whereby their graduates had each two votes, undemocratic? Yes, indeed. It was left to a Labor Government to abolish the university seats in 1946. Democracy could thenceforward reign unchallenged. It has, as we can all see, when someone who has never rubbed two thoughts together has as much *"say"* in the government of the country" as someone else who has bashed his brains until one or two o'clock in the small hours, to become a university graduate, or again to manage a small business in a place where he does

not reside. This was a notable triumph for "social justice."

2. The press. Even in 1814 the English press was positively first in the world. The American press was a poor, provincial or even parochial affair by comparison. The press created our public opinion. There was no *censorship* of news, as there was under Napoleon I in France and everywhere else. The notion that "the people" had to wait until 1934 for a popular press is, I rejoice to say, quite unfounded. My father read the *Daily News* in 1906. My wife's father read the *Daily Mail* (founded in 1896).

(Professor) W.R. Fryer
University of Nottingham

In the early eighteenth century, in the reign of Queen Anne, *The Spectator* flourished and Addison and Steele made an excellent living out of it. They wrote for the middle classes as well as the aristocracy. Addison's essays are in such first-class English and are so full of wit, erudition and good sense that we can still enjoy them. He and his companions are the grandsires of the modern news editors and owners. So also the old *Guardian* later, eighteenth century.

My dad's medical practice included many colliers' families. And I seem to remember that the coal miners and other working classes read the *Herald* when I was a boy (1911-1927) and they had others. Of course the lower classes enjoyed a feast of political lampoons and those doggerel pamphlets issued at public executions and other festive functions without any control or restraint from the ruling classes! (eighteenth and nineteenth centuries).

No doubt there has always been great competition for professorships. On the whole, the prestige of being *head of a college* at Oxford or Cambridge is greater than being a professor. (Every small college or university in the old and new worlds has professorships.) There is nepotism and jealousy in every walk of life, I believe: certainly in the judicial and legal worlds, and doubtless in the sphere of newspapermen?! It is no worse among academics, nor any less.

Perhaps C.S. Lewis was regarded as less promising in "administrative" ability? The duties of a professor, like a college head too, entail great administrative enthusiasm and diligence; he may (quite wrongly) have given an impression of casual indifference to the running of a faculty or branch of study?

Oxford has always accepted boys from humble homes. In the eighteenth century they were called servitors; they did domestic chores. There is a terrific camaraderie, and almost total lack of snobbery among undergraduates, although commoners like noblemen to share in activities. There is (and was) greater prestige in being a "scholar": a special gown and status with the fellows.

Cambridge we regarded in my day as virtually the same as Oxford, except that it was bigger with with fewer colleges. Oxford tended to be cosmopolitan and Cambridge "provincial." But generalization is always misleading—as is much of your article, I suspect.

I do not believe that Major W.H. Lewis took an Oxford degree. Nor that the Teamsters' Union in the United States is superior to the British Trade Unions. These are really useful bodies with *many* faults: one is to exaggerate the case against the bosses. (I had an uncle in the steel industry: he had an excellent relation with his work force; we used to go over the works.)

Reading your interesting article again, I question whether *all* dons ever want to become professors. It's like expecting all QC's (Queen's Counsels) to become judges. Lord Reith was a Puritan. At Oxford the Anglo-Catholics were a great force in the Colleges; and oddly enough they got on very well with the Puritan Congregationalists and Presbyterians. Lord Reith would not have allowed much of the vulgar, prurient rubbish we so often endure on BBC television today. I form the conclusion that some left-wing teacher has tried to mislead through theories based in biased opinions.

Maurice Mitchell-Heggs
Dunsfold, Surrey

Was C.S. Lewis prejudiced against Americans? In the final analysis, certainly not, I think; but on the way to the final analysis a few signposts are in order.

No one is free from the assumptions and the prejudices of his time. Lewis, though genetically he was Welsh-Scotch-Irish, received the upbringing and conditioning of an Edwardian Englishman. The Edwardian Englishman tended to make certain assumptions that have not stood the test of time (as well as some that have). He tended to be superior in his attitude towards women. Lewis's early letters show how unthinkingly he accepted this. Writing to his father on beginning his work as a lecturer in Oxford, he says something to the effect of, "The men come to see what my lectures are like, the women come to see what *I* am like." It seems not to have crossed his mind that a girl might study literature for its own sake, as he expected a boy to do. Later, this attitude was modified as Lewis's life brought him increasingly into contact with first-rate women scholars.

The Edwardian Englishman also tended to be anti-Semitic, at least to the extent that he regarded being a Jew as a social handicap; it seemed to him to be natural that a Jew, on attaining wealth, should take a non-Jewish name. As far as I know Lewis never showed a trace of this attitude. His innate decency saved him from it.

The Edwardian Englishman also patronized Americans. He called them "our American cousins," but always in a tone of voice that suggested that they were an inferior branch of the family somewhere in the remote provinces. Because their different historical tradition and different geographical situation had given them a different way of looking at things, the Edwardian Englishman found them quaint; since he made the untroubled assumption that there were two ways of looking at life: his own way and the wrong way. Americans, by definition, looked at life the wrong way.

This prejudice was particularly strong in traditional areas of education. Lewis had very definite ideas about what made an educated man. First and foremost, he had to have a good grounding in Latin and Greek; then, he had to know the English and French classics. Then, and only then, he entered the running.

The students with whom Lewis was dealing at Magdalen College in the 1920s and 30s came mostly from the English "Public" (i.e. private) schools and had been pretty well grounded in these things. Even when they were individually of very average intelligence, they had what Lewis regarded as the basic equipment. You didn't have to tell them who Aristotle was; if they ran across a passage in Latin or French, they could translate it at sight. American students, even when individually very bright, were often not so well grounded. I remember Edmund Wilson remarking to me that in his boyhood at the Hill School he had learned Latin and Greek, "but not so well as an English boy learns them." He was not complaining, merely stating what was to him an obvious fact.

If Lewis regarded American civilization as second-rate in those things he particularly valued, if he tended to comment approvingly on a writer and then add half-jokingly, "Pity he's an American," these attitudes were so common among his class and type as to excite no remark.

All this changed in later years. We must not give absolutely equal weight to Lewis's pronouncements from every period of his life. We must, as your contributor John L. Wright says (*Canadian C.S. Lewis Journal* Autumn 1982, p. 17), "grant him what we need to grant ourselves: the opportunity to grow in our understanding and experience."

America, up to 1941, was a vast backyard. The concerns of Americans were, overwhelmingly, domestic. It is true that the United States intervened decisively in the First World War; but this intervention came late, at a time when the European nations had bled themselves almost to death, and they remained unimpressed by the intervention and irritated by the claim sometimes made by Americans that they had "won the war." The Second World War was very different. Not only did it involve the large-scale mingling of populations for the first time, with the thousands of G.I.s quartered on British soil and the girls who subsequently married them, etc. It also meant the entrance of America on to the world stage, never to leave it. After that, while it was still possible to be venomously anti-American, as many Europeans still are, it was impossible to be merely patronizing. Lewis had the good sense to see this. It is also natural to suppose that, as an ex-soldier with experience of battle himself, he respected the courage and sacrifice of the American servicemen in the Pacific and Europe. And he responded to the individual generosity of Americans who sent food to British friends during the years of shortage in the later forties.

Meanwhile, American scholarship in the field of English literature was gathering authority, and Lewis was far too good a professional to ignore this. I particularly remember his speaking with admiration of Carl Young, author of *The Drama of the Mediaeval Church* (a book that obviously had a special interest for Lewis).

I made Lewis's acquaintance when I was his pupil during the war years, and in the immediate post-war period I was an inconspicuous member of his circle, the Inklings. I had at that time a keen interest in American poetry; during the war, when we could not get American books at all, a whole generation of American poets had been producing interesting work, and I would sometimes share my discoveries with the Inklings. A poet of whom Lewis had never heard, and to whose work I introduced him, was John Crowe Ransom. Lewis was very taken with the Ransom poems I read to him, especially "Captain Carpenter." Ransom was, in fact, a man of about Lewis's own age, who had studied at Oxford as a Rhodes Scholar, and the two of them might perfectly well have met—but they never had; and Lewis's unconsciousness of Ransom's existence may perhaps take us back to the point at which we began—that Lewis's generation, in their younger days, took very little notice of America or Americans.

I am certain that this attitude changed in later years; and I am glad to think that, on the literary side, I may have contributed my own little bit towards changing it.

John Wain
Oseney, Oxford

Another graduate of Oxford and pupil of Lewis's, Charles Wrong, who has been teaching history at the University of South Florida for about fifteen years, writes as follows:

"I did not at first believe Lewis *was* prejudiced against Americans. But the prejudice is revealed in *They Stand Together: The Letters of C.S. Lewis to Arthur Greeves*. But this is the expression of a young man's still fairly immature views. When, in the thirties, Lewis writes to Greeves about his student's lack of competence, that may reflect, not any kind of antipathy but simply a judgment of her abilities. It is widely believed in Europe that most American scholarship is hopelessly superficial. They just don't have the necessary knowledge. My own experience does a good deal to bear this out. The quality of written work done by most of my students, even education majors—especially education majors—and even in their senior year, would not pass muster in England in the fourth form of a grammar school; and in France would get much shorter shrift than that. Yes, I know these are undergraduates and Lewis's student was a graduate. But there seems to be a prevailing acceptance of slipshod work all the way through the American academic world.

"You speak of 'the English, coming after the Spanish and French and thus thwarted of much mineral wealth,' and they considered the colonies 'an outlet for social sewage.' There is plenty of mineral wealth in North America now, of course. But I don't think either the English or anyone else cared in those days about nickel. What they were after was gold and silver. And only the Spanish found bullion; I never heard of the French doing so. The English colonists hoped, some of them anyway, to come across new Mexicos and Perus; so did the Spaniards who explored places like Arizona. But they didn't start colonizing until the seventeenth century, and surely only the wildest optimists can have believed that there were finds of gold and silver still to be made. (Of course, California in the 1840s would prove these optimists right. But were the colonists in Virginia or Massachusetts really hoping to find gold and silver?)

"Then, the reference to 'social sewage.' I'm sure the government in London regarded many of the colonists as so much riff-raff. But your phrase gives the impression that people like the Pilgrim Fathers were deliberately dumped across the Atlantic to get them out of the way. In fact, they went on their own accord; and the government not only didn't encourage their going but disliked it, and thought of forbidding it. (Charles I did, I believe, forbid Cromwell to emigrate!) Of course, whether the colonists in the seventeenth century were carefully screened by the government (as the French who went to Canada were) or were a bunch of awkward customers getting away from a government and social order they resented (as the English settlers were), doesn't have much bearing on why Lewis should have disliked their descendants three centuries later. I think the nub of the matter is the reference to the 'real discoverer of America being greed.' This is something that I have long believed to be a fact, and I try (tactfully, I hope) to suggest it to my classes.

"Europeans saw the New World as a place where they could get rich in a hurry. Americans—and Canadians too, I imagine—soon got the reputation of being very good at working for themselves— enterprising, hard-working, and independent—but very bad at working for anybody else. But the object of working for yourself was to get rich.

The tradition seems to linger. The thing for the individual American to do is to grow rich, and it doesn't greatly matter how. Getting rich is what being an American is all about. You remember what Screwtape says to Wormwood: 'My good is my good, and your good is yours.' There are times when I think Screwtape is alive and well and making it big on the American scene. It may have been this that Lewis disliked. Of course, to be fair, he was also used to a traditionalist, class-oriented society, and he may have resented the fact that American society was different.

"I don't know how Lewis felt. I never discussed the subject with him. Norman Bradshaw knew him much better than I did. And if Norman says that his prejudice against Americans disappeared as a result of their kindness during and after the war, and as a result of meeting far more individual Americans, I'm sure Norman is right."

About your article, "Oxford Loses a Genius," it seems to me that truth is mixed with irrelevancies. The (hereditary) aristocracy is not the same at all as the intellectual élite. It was the intellectual élite that Lewis offended. The Chancellor of Oxford is only a figurehead, always a peer, not in residence, irrelevant to anything. The Vice-Chancellor is head of the University. If there was an oligarchy at Oxford, it was the intellectual élite, not the real aristocracy.

The hierarchical horse that has trotted through England for centuries (as you say) is the real aristocracy, not the intellectual élite, which has become important only in the nineteenth and twentieth centuries. They were the ones who always said, and still do (not only at Oxford and Cambridge but also at Yale and Harvard and Chicago): "Power should *not* be in the hands of aristocrats or politicians but in the hands of intellectuals." They were the ones who were not only against Lewis; they did him in on the professorship.

The confusion in your article between the genuine aristocracy and the intellectuals is, then, one point. Lord David Cecil, to be sure, is an aristocrat, like Churchill's father, the younger son of a duke; but he is a genuine scholar: at Oxford his claim to fame was not his blood or courtesy title but his scholarship. Anyhow, he was on Lewis's side. Still, the Oxford and Cambridge intellectuals *were* part of the Establishment, a vague term for "the powers," political or otherwise: the people who run things.

If Lewis lost the Professorship of Poetry by only nineteen votes, then roughly half of the dons voted for him. Lewis ought to have had the Professorship of English Literature or Mediaeval Literature. You say the Professorship of Poetry is "usually given to critics, sometimes to scholars." You may be right; but I doubt it: rarely, I think, to critics, if ever. And usually, I think, to *poets.* C.S. Lewis was a poet, but not esteemed as such. C. Day Lewis *was* esteemed as a poet (though I don't think much of his poetry). There was lots of talk at the time that it should have been given to W.H. Auden, as, I think, it later was. Or Stephen Spender.

On the other hand, it was commonly said that no man knew as much about English literature as Lewis. And I repeat, if nearly half (nineteen-vote difference) voted for him, your frequent condemnation of "Oxford" or "educated Oxonians" or "senior Oxonians" is a bit unfair to those, including the highly educated and senior Oxonians like Tolkien and Lord David and many others, who were *for* C.S. Lewis.

The double vote of MAs of Oxford or Cambridge (virtually all the graduates), a vote for their local MP and a vote for the University MP—each university had one—may not be egalitarian, but I've never approved of anything more. I see no reason why a citizen should not be able to achieve extra votes (as John Stuart Mill suggested) by attainments. Modern egalitarianism says a docker is equal to the don or a duke, and two dockers are superior to the don or the duke. Read Nevill Shute's novel, *In the Wet.* Anyway, the double vote is *totally* irrelevant to your article.

Another point in your article seems a bit confused. An Oxford don is a fellow of a *college,* a tutor. C.S. Lewis was a fellow of Magdalen, for life. As Mr. Mitchell-Heggs remarks in his letter in the same issue, "Most dons do not want to become professors; nor need they be to become 'powers.' *Some* dons also accept additional jobs from the *University* as readers or lecturers (which are equivalent ranks to assistant and associate professors in the U.S. universities). But in each field there is only *one* Professor (hence far more prestigious than the U.S. "full" professorship): one professor of Welsh literature, one professor of Modern English literature, etc., and no one can be given that chair unless the incumbent dies or retires.

But they can create a new chair as the Professorship of Poetry may have originally been. A newly created chair is *not* less of an honor than an old, established one; and if specially created for one man, as the Cambridge chair was for Lewis, may be more of an honor. But, note, the wicked Oxonians in your article *did* try to get Lewis back and make amends with a chair after Cambridge had shown the way!

Your point about the BBC and newspapers for the masses may be true. And certainly the masses should have something that gives them the news in simple sentences. But I've always thought, and still do, that papers and broadcasters who cater to the *taste* of the masses—taste for juicy sex scandals, etc.—are wrong. The BBC's idea of programs a *little* above the taste of the masses, I approve of.

Pusey and Keble were more than mere clergymen inasmuch as they were household words and leaders along with Newman of the famous Oxford Movement. May I say I think Mr. Mitchell-Heggs's last paragraph is right.

There is *some* truth to the idea that Oxford and Cambridge felt themselves to be the intellectual centers of England (as they were and are). Scholarly books may overturn long-held theories or throw light, new light, on a subject from that time on. Plato and Aristotle shaped Western civilization; but the Athenian "masses" didn't read them.

Lewis was a scholar. *The Allegory of Love* was a profound and brilliant scholarly book, almost revolutionary in the new light it cast upon its subject. It's the sort of book that the universities exist to produce—their *main* reason for existing. Only secondary is the aim of educating the young. Not unreasonably, Oxford feels that its dons should get on with scholarship and tutoring and not spend half their time writing for the *Daily Mail;* for if they do, they are only half-time scholars, if at all. This is the basis for their attitude toward C.S. Lewis. Popular novels are all very well; but a scholar hasn't the time. *Some* truth, you see.

So Lewis, who had proved himself a brilliant scholar, ought not, they said, to be taking the many, many hours to write and do on the BBC things like 'Broadcast Talks,' as well as writing *The Screwtape Letters* and science fiction, because these were hours that didn't go into scholarship, which he was superbly equipped to do. He was letting the University and the world of scholarship down.

But, you may say, Lewis did much else of brilliance and scholarship. Yes, of course. But the critics would say that he could have done still more, much more. Perhaps he could have; but, in view of the fact that his scholarly accomplishments were greater than those of many full-time scholars, the criticism is without much weight.

The other reason, far greater in my opinion, is the matter of Christianity. If Lewis had written witty, dark-blue detective stories under a pseudonym (though everyone would know who it was), he would probably not have lost the professorships. The matter of Christianity was at the bottom of the ever-deepening chasm between orthodox Christianity—what the Christians have always believed—and the "liberal" or "modernist" or secularizing semi-Christianity.

Intellectuals (not all, but many) were accepting the idea that it was not intellectually respectable to believe in a *real* Resurrection, feeling that other intellectuals had somehow disproved such things. (They *had not* disproved them; and the dons who thought they had, knew no more about it than businessmen or army officers—it was simply an intellectual "climate" of disbelief.) Anyway, these semi-Christians, modernist and liberal, were not only outraged at Lewis for writing popular books but for writing popular books that asserted the truth of "outmoded" orthodoxy. Whatever fury there was (actually not great fury) over his writing of *popular* books was tripled, quadrupled, by their being popular books that proclaimed the *Faith*. (Lewis himself has shown in *That Hideous Strength* and in his address "The Inner Ring," what he was up against. The Inner Ring of Oxford was against him, the innermost ring.)

Make no mistake about it. Christ was at the center of the war. The Oxonian hatred was the same as the hatred expressed in The *New York Times*.[28] "What think ye of Christ?" When dons explained their opposition to Lewis as being his writing of popular books, they were covering up their real opposition to Christ. One doesn't say, "I hate and reject Christ"; one votes against Lewis.

And make no mistake about this either: Lewis's heart was *always* in Oxford, despite Cambridge.

You are dead right about the immense irony of an Oxford, founded by the Catholic Church, everything named Jesus and Corpus Christi and Christ Church and Lewis's own (Mary) Magdalen, voting down its great Christian.

Sheldon Vanauken
Lynchburg, Virginia

Editor's note: I thank Mr. Vanauken for such a valuable letter; but one or two points need to be clarified.

Mr. Vanauken says that I regard some Oxonians as "wicked" or look upon them "with contempt." I did not mean that. No. The salient fact is that Lewis knew more about English and poetry than anyone else in Oxford. A pupil of C.S. Lewis's told me that. A distinguished Oxonian aristocrat told me that Lewis was the greatest, and then added, "by *far* the greatest man he had known in Oxford in all his years there." Unquestionably, Lewis was great. That is point one.

Point two is this. After two or three years of fooling around in science and engineering, I flunked out of McGill University. I hardly read a book at all until about the age of twenty-six, when all my friends were away at war—I was rejected, too deaf for active service—and loneliness induced me to discover the wonders of the printed word. I read O. Henry, de Maupassant, Thomas Wolfe. Much of Lewis's *Preface to Paradise Lost* is beyond my comprehension. But much of it I understand well. I can see clearly that that work far transcends anything ever written about Milton and his work. And surely that *Preface to Paradise Lost,* especially together with *The Allegory of Love,* merits a professorship. Even I can see that.

Quite apart from the voting of MAs, the gentlemen of Oxford empowered to promote could have offered him a vacancy or a created chair. They did not. For nineteen years after his genius was recognized, he was ignored. Thus it is obvious that educated Oxonians can be as readily vindictive as uneducated politicians or the mere wolves of Broadway. I do not, please understand, regard them with contempt or as villains. I am simply surprised and sorry for them. I thought that they of all people, believer and atheist, presumably intellectual elite enjoying "the highly selective consciousness of fully alert men," would be above such behavior. I was wrong. The truth is that *A Preface to Paradise Lost* was published in 1942. Oxford finally offered Lewis a professorship in 1957. Fifteen years! That is a long time to hold an apple under a horse's nose.

—Editor

Your unexpected letter tickled me pink, as the Americans say. In his *Analects,* Confucius says, "A friend comes from afar, is it not delightful?" It is really good to hear from a C.S. Lewis lover in a faraway land. You ask of my own impressions of his books? He is my spiritual mentor; I owe him so much that it is impossible to write my impressions in a letter or two.

You may be interested to know that I recently met and talked with Charles Colson, the American worker for prison reform. He was a bit surprised when I mentioned having translated Lewis's *Mere Christianity* (which had changed Colson's life), and was writing a Japanese book on Lewis. Mr. Colson stayed in Japan for a week or so, giving lectures and visiting prisons here and there.

(Professor) Naoyuki Yagyu
Kanto Gakuin University
Yokohama

C.S. Lewis was so kind to me at a rather bad time of my life. When I was young I lost my husband, then had an illness and was told I could not live. On top of that I was told my little daughter was likely to be mentally defective. I did not die, and as my son was at a good school, and my daughter needed a great deal of medical attention, I went to Oxford to read social science. It was there that I met Mr. Lewis. Someone mentioned Mr. Lewis to me, and *The Screwtape Letters*. From the book I knew that Mr. Lewis must know almost everything about human beings that it was possible to know. I found that clergymen were nearly always un-understanding people. I wrote to Mr. Lewis and asked if I could talk to him. Immediately I received a note from him at Magdalen College, suggesting that I come to see him. I went to his room. And I could not believe that this now famous man, was sitting with an old slipper dangling from his foot, and that his pullover was a little holey. He had a kind rosy face, and reminded me so much of the nice homely farmers of my home surroundings.

Mr. Lewis and I were soon chatting and I told him how unhappy I was; and how desperately anxious about my children. I mentioned that it was because of *The Screwtape Letters* that I thought he would understand that I was genuine, and needed kindness. He then told me how funny it was that he had tried over and over again to write something that he could get across; and then quite suddenly he had awakened one morning to find himself famous. He said that if I had an urge to write, I must go on and on; and in fact I would find I had to. I asked him how he knew so much about human beings, as to be able to write *The Screwtape Letters*. He smiled and said, "I only had to know myself really well."

From then on life became easier at Oxford. I visited Mr. Lewis occasionally, and when I went down once, I had another blow, a lawsuit . . . . I wrote in some distress to Mr. Lewis, for advice and I suppose comfort. He wrote back saying he had established a fund to help people in trouble, and he would contribute towards the cost of a defence. The case, however, was dropped. But this incident let me know that Mr. Lewis had established a fund to help people.

Mr. Lewis was a good friend, and is one of my happy memories. I should like him to know that I qualified as a social worker and became the boarding out officer for my county. My daughter became well and married. My son has a good job, and is married with two children. I suppose Mr. Lewis knows this. And I hope he knows how much he helped me when I was almost desperate.

(Mrs.) Joan B. Pile
England

My trouble with Lewis is that I rarely want to read any other writer. I keep rereading him. I think as you progress in your Lewis education each book reread takes on a new and clearer meaning. It is lovely to be able to write to a total stranger and feel, because of the common bond, that we can be totally in communication. Lewis opened up a whole new world to me; and, as he said of George MacDonald and also of his tutor, Kirkpatrick, I owe him more than any words can express. I did not realize how really universal some things about myself were, and somehow felt so much better. It is not for nothing that God had him write the books he did instead of the ones he could have written of a more learned nature and thereby follow his field and advance himself. I am so grateful for and how he wrote. He introduced me to Charles Williams, George MacDonald, G.K. Chesterton, and others. "My imagination has been baptized"—another one of his quotes. Never again can I live and enjoy the same old things. I see *winter* especially— and all outdoors—with a new vision. Lewis had an uncanny awareness of what went on inside a person. Now, when I meet someone I immediately wonder what manner of man this is. I do not see the externals, but realize there *is* much more. It makes for a friendliness towards people I could not have had otherwise.

(Mrs.) Loring Ellis
Hampton, South Carolina

It is convenient to add here my own few letters from Lewis.

I suppose I wrote to him a dozen—possibly twenty—times in as many years. Stupidly, I threw away most of his answers, sometimes quite long, always prompt and straight to the point. Below are the few I kept. The first letter (August 23, 1956) answers my query: Why does God allow war, and how can soldiers condone killing? (Apparently he had mail forwarded while on holiday in Ireland.)

Dear Mr. Schofield,

One must distinguish "approving absolutely" from "approving as the lesser evil under certain conditions." All war, like all lawsuits, results from greed, selfishness, or ill faith on one side or both. Therefore God disapproves of them. But granted that someone's greed, selfishness or ill faith, has started the thing, does God think the work of a good soldier or a good lawyer a less evil than letting the aggressor have his way?

From the fact that neither St. John the Baptist nor Christ disapproved of soldiers as such, I conclude that the answer is Yes.

By the Christian ideal of the Christian at arms in a just cause I mean the Knight as he is pictured in all the romances of the Middle Ages.

Yours sincerely,
C.S. Lewis

On tour in Eire
August 23, 1956

The second letter (February 26, 1959) refers to Mere Christianity *(III, 3) in which he writes: "There are to be no passengers or parasites. If a man does not work, he ought not to eat. Every one is to work with his own hands, and every one's work is to produce something good. There will be no manufacture of silly luxuries and then of sillier advertisements to persuade us to buy them." I asked him where he got that.*

1z8/59

The Kilns,Kiln Lane,
Headington Quarry,
Oxford.
26th February 1959.

Dear Mr Schofield,

Thanks for your letter,and I am so glad that you find some comfort in Mere Christianity.

The reference you want is second Thessalonians,Chapter III.

With all good wishes,

yours sincerely,

C. S. Lewis

*In Oxford on a honeymoon, I tried in vain to see him at Magdalen.
He was out. I left a note with the porter. Lewis had actually married the
same year. But I didn't know.*

56/128

Magdalene College,
Cambridge.
10th October 1956.

Dear Schofield,

Thanks for your letter of the 7th, which did not reach
me until this morning. Sorry to have missed you, but Cambridge term
began yesterday, so I fear there is no chance of a meeting.
Congratulations on your marriage, and with best wishes for your
happiness,

yours sincerely,

C. S Lewis

From Quebec I sent Lewis a tin of maple syrup and some honey. He
replied:

As from Magdalene College
Cambridge
31 January '60

Dear Mr. Schofield

Your parcel arrived on Saturday. You could not have chosen a
better present. My wife (who is an American) loves maple syrup and, as
it is a pretty rare commodity, her heart leaped up as yours or mine would
at the sight of white man's food in the depths of China. And we all like
honey. It is really extraordinarily kind of you not only to buy these
dainties but to think of it and go through all the Red Tape. Hearty
thanks. It is like spring here today and the first snowdrops and crocuses
are already coming up.

With all grateful greetings—the alliteration came unasked.

Yours sincerely,
C.S. Lewis

196

Of course I had no knowledge that his wife had died about six weeks before I sent this note:

```
                    "Vann,"
                    Hambledon, Godalming,
                    Surrey.
                    July 26, 1960.



Dear Dr. Lewis,

            May I please have
your permission to quote a few
lines from chap. 8, book III, of
"Mere Christianity" for a
newspaper article?

            And with every
good wish indeed, I am,


                    Sincerely,

                    S. Schofield.
                    S. Schofield.
```

Certainly. With compliments.

C. S. L.

And two subsequent letters from his brother, Major W.H. Lewis:

"Letters of C.S. Lewis", a book
edited by his brother, W.H. Lewis

The Kilns, Kiln Lane,
Headington Quarry,
Oxford.
21st July 1967.

Dear Mr. Schofield,

You make me blush by your praise of the Letters and of my share in their presentation; but I am none the less pleased that you should have thought so well of them.

Yes, his capacity for writing sympathetically to all sorts of people with so many kinds of problems was astonishing - and the care with which he turned from his own heavy work to deal with each. I acted as his secretary for many years, and looking back, I am surprised at the small number of letters he let me draft for his signature - hardly ever any except those dealing with trivialities.

If his Oxford days were not for him entirely happy ones, he felt more than compensated by his short tenure of the Cambridge Chair; at Cambridge he felt almost at once in his proper element both socially and professionally and indeed I think he regretted that he had not in 1917 decided on Camb--ridge in preference to Oxford.

As regards the Oxford Poetry Chair I was given to understand that there were wheels within wheels. He was by no means universally popular here. There were people in Oxford, important and self-important, who were Unknown in the outside world, and not a few of whom bitterly resented the fact that Jack had a following to whom his tenure of a Fellowship at Oxford was a minor detail of his career. Hinc illae lacrimae.

As regards his loathing for hymns, I think the saving 'almost' must have meant that he liked some as poetry - Herbert's for example. But he most certainly disliked any hymn singing, though he would have been shocked and indignant at its suppression on aesthetic grounds.

I was much touched by your expression of sympathy with me, for his is a loss which I shall feel to the end of my days. Lamb has said the last word about this kind of loss - the joke that you can share with only one person, and he has gone from you - the view which he would have appreciated - and so on. But, as I put on his tombstone (after a demur from the parson who urged something from the Bible) 'Men must endure their going hence'.

With many thanks,

yours sincerely,

W.H. LEWIS.

The Kilns,Kiln Lane,
Headington Quarry,
Oxford.
4th September 1967.

Dear Mr.Schofield,

        Thanks for your letter of the 1st.and for the book. The
latter I have not got round to reading yet,but it looks interesting and I
will see that it is safely returned when I've finished it.

Yes,time does soften grief,mercifully. But I often miss him still - the
little daily things which I could tell him and which he only would have
enjoyed. I particularly miss him on Sunday evenings when I would dearly
like to have his comments on his own 'Lion,Witch,and Wardrobe',which is
now running as a TV serial. Done reverently and well I think,with a quite
remarkable 'Lucy',in real life a girl of twelve and a great little actress

I am very grateful to you for your kind invitation,but I don't get about
very much these days; after all I'm in my 73rd.year and travel no longer
has the fascination for me it once had. But if I'm on the move I will be
more than pleased to pay you a visit. I except I'd find Surrey sadly
changed these days. When I was eighteen I crammed for Sandhurst at the
tiny Surrey village of Great Bookham,an idyllic place in lovely country;
I suppose today it has 'developed' into one of London's huge dormitories.

A copy of the photo you want leaves by today's post,and of course you have
my permission to make use of it. I should think you will also want that of
the photographer,and this you will find on the back of the print.

If and when you are in Oxford,do look me up. I need 24 hours notice to
provide a meal,this being a batchelor establishment and my housekeeper
being a devotee of the 'day to day' system of feeding.

With all good wishes,

                     yours sincerely,

                     W.H.LEWIS.

Photograph by W. Suschitzky

C.S. LEWIS

Epilogue

I saw Lewis again in Oxford, a few days after our lunch together. There was no mistaking his ruddy face and bright brown eyes. Wearing a cloth hat, the same tweed jacket and baggy flannels, he was in front of University College, walking towards Magdalen Bridge. I stopped to greet him, "Hello, Mr. Lewis! You had me in for lunch the other day—remember?"

I stopped, but something restrained me. I could not catch his eye. He was looking up and far away. As he passed I turned and followed his gaze which appeared to focus on the top of Magdalen Tower. Swinging a stout stick, his gait a comfortable amble, he crossed the bridge and disappeared into the crowd.

Notes

Chapter One
Part B: Exhilaration
Kenneth Tynan

1. Bailey, with a major in Greek from Columbia University, became Russian and German liaison officer to Eisenhower's deputy, General Walter Bedell Smith, at SHAEF; he served as interpreter and translator at the surrender in Berlin. Subsequently he became Lewis's pupil and graduated with a BA and MA from Oxford University in 1949.

2. April 23, 1964, quoted with permission.

3. *C.S. Lewis: Speaker and Teacher,* edited by Carolyn Keefe (Zondervan, US, 1973; Hodder and Stoughton, UK, 1974).

4. Ibid.

5. *The Reporter,* April 23, 1964, and *C.S. Lewis: Speaker and Teacher* (Zondervan, US, 1971; Hodder and Stoughton, UK, 1974), edited by Carolyn Keefe, p. 114.

6. *English Literature in the Sixteenth Century, Excluding Drama.* Vol. III, The Oxford History of English Literature (Oxford University Press, 1954; paperback, Penquin [now out-of-print] 1973).

7. *C.S. Lewis: Speaker and Teacher,* edited by Carolyn Keefe (Zondervan, US, 1971; Hodder and Stoughton, UK, 1974), p. 114.

8. See *Reflections on the Psalms* (Fontana, UK, 1971; Harcourt, Brace, Jovanovich, US) IX, "A Word about Praising," p. 77.

9. *Miracles,* (Collins, UK, paperback 1980; Macmillan, US, 1947).

10. Oxford University Press, UK and US, 1971.

Chapter Two
The Butcher
Alan Rook
1. Routledge and Sons, London.
2. Ibid.
3. Ibid.
4. The Inklings were a group of friends who met in Lewis's rooms on Friday evenings. Tea was served. One or two would read chapters from forthcoming books. Judgment was always frank. The Inklings were the first to hear J.R.R. Tolkien's *The Lord of the Rings.* Lewis's *The Problem of Pain* is dedicated "To the Inklings"; and in a letter[4*] he mentions four Inklings who provided him with "incalculable help"— Hugo Dyson, Charles Williams, Tolkien, and R. Havard, his doctor. In the words of John Wain, the Inklings were a group of instigators, almost of incendiaries, meeting to urge one another on in the task of redirecting the whole current of contemporary art and life.[4†] Humphrey Carpenter, Tolkien's biographer,[4§] has written a very well-received book entitled *The Inklings* (Houghton Mifflin, Boston; Allen and Unwin, London; Methuen, Toronto, 1980, hardback and paperback). Oh, yes, there is a little joke about his writing of this book. Mr. Carpenter spent a week on research at the Wade Collection at Wheaton College, Illinois. "For there," he tells me, "are several hundred letters of Charles Williams to his wife; Major W.H. Lewis's diaries which record many Inklings' sessions; the letters of C.S. Lewis to his brother during the 1930s and 1940s, and much else of interest. Professor Clyde Kilby (who built the collection) was away while I was there. But the staff made me feel welcome in the nicest possible way. And my visit was a time of friendship and delight, as well as study." So here we have an Englishman writing a most English book, having to travel four-thousand miles to the middle of the United States to discover how a group of Englishmen behaved in England.
4*. *Letters of C.S. Lewis,* December 21, 1941.
4†. See *Sprightly Running* (Macmillan, UK and US, 1965), pp. 181 and 185.
4§. *J.R.R. Tolkien: A Biography* (Allen and Unwin, UK; Houghton Mifflin, US, 1977).
5. See *Enid Starkie* by Joanna Richardson (Murray, UK; Macmillan,

US, 1973), p. 188.

6. *I Call it Joy: C.S. Lewis Remembered,* BBC, January 29, 1978.

7. A "tube" is colloquial English for an underground train.

Chapter Three
Impressions of a Pupil
Norman Bradshaw

1. Published in Belfast, Ireland, 1897; on sale at Blackwell's Bookshop, Oxford, in 1974, for £10.

2. Mr. Rowse's latest book is *A Cornishman Abroad* (Cape, London, 1976); this is the third volume of his autobiographical writings, following *A Cornish Childhood* and *A Cornishman at Oxford.*

3. *The Allegory of Love* (Oxford University Press, UK and US, 1958), pp. 16-17.

4. *The Pilgrim's Regress* (Bles, UK; Eerdmans, US), p. 52.

5. *A Grief Observed* (under pseudonym of N.W. Clerk, Faber, UK, 1961; Seabury, US, 1963; as by C.S. Lewis, Faber, Seabury, 1964).

6. *The Four Loves* (Bles, UK; Harcourt, Brace, Jovanovich, US, 1960).

7. Supporting this story is an item in the new book, *Brothers and Friends.* The Lewis brothers were dining at the home of fairly new friends, Mr. and Mrs. Hugo Dyson. And Mrs. Dyson had invited another lady to balance up the party. "After dinner," says Major Lewis, "things improved considerably. Dyson took us to a little book lined study, where we had coffee and he read an imitation of Pope, and which I thought good, tho' I was handicapped by not understanding most of the allusions . . . . I was just getting comfortable when he uttered the fatal 'Shall we join the ladies?' which put me out more, as I had not been expecting it. (J afterwards said, 'I wonder what would have happened if one had just said Well, I think we're very comfortable where we are')." *Brothers and Friends: An Intimate Portrait of C.S. Lewis: The Diaries of Major Warren Hamilton Lewis,* edited by Clyde S. Kilby and Marjorie Lamp Mead (Harper & Row, 1982), p. 99.

8. *Letters of C.S. Lewis,* edited and with a memoir by W.H. Lewis; (Bles, UK, Harcourt, Brace, Jovanovich, 1966), letter dated March 13, 1921, p. 55.

9. *The Lamp-Post* of the Southern California C.S. Lewis Society, Vol. 1, No. 4, Oct. 1977, p. 5.

10. *The Problem of Pain* (Fontana, UK; Macmillan, US, 1975).

11. *Miracles* (Fontana, UK, 1974; Macmillan, US).

12. Each soul may be a product of heredity and environment, but that only means that heredity and environment are among the instruments whereby God creates a soul. (See *The Problem of Pain*, Chapter X, "Heaven.")

13. Oxford University Press, UK and US, 1958.

14. *Letters of C.S. Lewis*, p. 83.

15. John Wain in *The American Scholar*, winter issue 1980-1981.

16. *The Pilgrim's Regress* (Sheed and Ward, UK, 1935; Eerdmans, US, 1958), p. 162, in the 1935 Sheed and Ward issue.

17. Ibid., p. 207.

18. Ibid., p. 255.

19. *Surprised by Joy: The Shape of My Early Life* (Harcourt, Brace, Jovanovich, US, 1956).

Chapter Four
Disappointment at Cambridge?
W.R. Fryer

1. *Mere Christianity*, II, 2.

2. Ibid.

3. Romans 8:38, 39 (*The New English Bible*, Oxford University Press, Cambridge University Press, 1961). It is curious that when one of President Nixon's closest confidants, Charles Colson, was in court and about to be sentenced to prison, these same verses from Romans came to his mind. Never, he says, had they been more important to him. See *Born Again* (Chosen Books, US; Hodder and Stoughton, UK, 1976), p. 207.

4. *Light on C.S. Lewis* (Bles, UK, 1965), p. 77. See also *C.S. Lewis: a Biography* by Roger Lancelyn Green and Walter Hooper (Collins, UK, 1972; Harcourt, Brace, Jovanovich, US, 1972), p. 289.

Chapter Five
C.S. Lewis, the Teacher
E.L. Edmonds

1. About Beatrix Potter, Professor Edmonds says, "I met her in the most extraordinary circumstances. I had always had a great admiration for Wordsworth, ever since the day when, at the ripe old age of eight

years, I had stood on my seat in the classroom of the local village school and recited 'Daffodils.'

"In my mid-teens I made a pilgrimage to Wordsworth's countryside, declaiming yards of his poetry beside the tarns he loved so well. There was nothing original in this: Wordsworth and Coleridge had done something similar years before. I remember swimming in one of the tarns and being very nearly drowned when I got the cramps whilst out of my depth. Though aware of Hazlitt's dictum about 'never less alone than when alone,' I occasionally had a strange sensation of the presence of another (probably because Wordsworth had also mentioned this more than once).

"I was coming back late one afternoon when it began to rain heavily, as it can in the hills, so I took, as I thought, a hasty short-cut across the fields. I was suddenly accosted by a stumpy old lady with what looked like an old sack spread about her shoulders. She was obviously very cross (and startled too) and I thought immediately of 'gypsy country.' I fled black along the way I had come, got lost, and only arrived back very wet in the late evening at the farmhouse in Near Sawrey where I was staying.

"I was then told it was only Mrs. Heelis, better known as Beatrix Potter, and that the land was indeed hers—Hill Top Farm.

"I have been a great admirer of hers ever since. Lewis and I discussed aspects of her style with great gusto. My only regret is that I never went back to apologize to her."

2. *Kaggy* (and its variants) means "left," e.g. in cricket kaggy-handed is left-handed; a kaggy bowler is a left-handed bowler.

3. *Mizzy* in Lancashire dialect means "marsh" or "marshy."

4. *Greyfriars* refers to a whole series of stories about life in a boys' public (boarding) school. The magazine ran for years, and the psychology of the boys was attractively simplistic: a romantic loyalty to the code, no matter what, and good must triumph in the end. Rather like so many of Dickens's characters, good boys were patently good, bad ones clearly bad; and there were the in-between ones like Billy Bunter, the fat boy who was always getting in (and out of) scrapes.

5. *The master indeed of them that know!* An echo of Dante's original reference (to Aristotle) in the Divine Comedy: "Il Maestro di color che sanno."

Chapter Six
Part A: With Girls at Home
Partricia Heidelberger
1. Mrs. Moore was Lewis's adopted mother.

Chapter Seven
Part A: With Women at College
Rosamund Cowan
1. Owen Barfield, to the editor, London, March 2, 1977.
2. In an unpublished letter to Delmar Banner.
3. *Letters of C.S. Lewis* (July 1, 1921), p. 64.
4. Homer: The *Iliad,* translated by E.V. Rieu (Penguin, sixteenth impression, 1967), p. xvi. It is noteworthy that [Lord] Kenneth Clark mentions the same point: "In spite of recent triumphs of science, men haven't changed much in the last two thousand years." See *Civilisation* (British Broadcasting Corporation and John Murray, London, sixth impression, 1970), last page.
5. *Broadcast Talks.* published in the US as *The Case for Christianity,* are now incorporated in *Mere Christianity.*
6. *Miracles* has long since been a book (Collins paperback, London, 1980; Macmillan paperback, 1980).

Chapter Seven
Part B: With Women at College
Patricia Thomson
1. The four books are *Sir Thomas Wyatt and His Background* (Routledge and Kegan Paul, London; Stanford University Press, California); *Elizabethan Lyrical Poets* (Routledge and Kegan Paul, 1967); *Collected Poems of Sir Thomas Wyatt,* edited by Kenneth Muir and Patricia Thomson (Liverpool University Press, 1969); and *Wyatt: The Central Heritage* (Routledge and Kegan Paul, 1974).

Chapter Seven
Part D: With Women at College
Muriel Jones
1. *A Preface to Paradise Lost* (Oxford University Press, UK and US, 1972).

2. *Letters of C.S. Lewis,* edited and with a memoir by W.H. Lewis (Bles, UK; Harcourt, Brace, Jovanovich, US, 1966), letter dated December 21, 1941.

3. *Transposition and Other Addresses* (Bles, UK, 1949) and as *The Weight of Glory and Other Addresses* (Macmillan, US, 1949; paperback, Eerdmans, US).

Chapter Eight
Reactions From Other Women
Kathryn Lindskoog

1. This whole letter, which is quite long, is in Mrs. Lindskoog's book, *The Lion of Judah in Never-Never Land* (Eerdmans, Grand Rapids, Michigan, 1973).

2. *Letters of C.S. Lewis* (December 20, 1961), p. 301.

3. Ibid.

4. *C.S. Lewis: Speaker and Teacher,* edited by Carolyn Keefe (Zondervan, 1971; Hodder and Stoughton, London, 1973).

Chapter Nine
A Guest in the House
George Sayer

1. Spend as little as possible on himself? His housekeepers, Molly and Leonard Miller, told me he once asked, "When you go to town would you please get me a pair of gloves at Woolworth's?"

"Oh, *no,* Mr. Jack," she said, "Not *Woolworth's,* not for *you?*"

"Yes," he said, "that's all I can afford. Here's sixpence."

Chapter Ten
South African View
Peter Philip

1. Peter Philip's brother, David, now a publisher in Cape Town, was also a pupil of Lewis's. David Philip tells me that when he first arrived in Oxford, "I saw a ruddy-faced farmer trudging through Magdalen grounds in a bulky tweed suit and Wellington boots and with a sack of what looked like potatoes on his back. It was explained to me that this was C.S. Lewis with a bag of books."

2. *Digs* is colloquial English for a boarding house.

Chapter Eleven
Stunning Effect
Erik Routley

1. Reprinted with permission of Dr. Routley and C.S. Lewis: *The Bulletin of the New York C.S. Lewis Society,* vol. 4, no. 3, January, 1973 issue.
2. Charles Williams was a writer and editor for Oxford University Press, which had been in London and moved to Oxford during the war. Lewis introduced him to the Inklings and arranged for him to lecture at the University. When I asked Major Lewis what Charles Williams was like, he said, "Personally, he was charming, and professionally, he was the kind of man who naturally rose to the top." When Williams died, C.S. Lewis referred to him as his friend of friends.
3. "The Weight of Glory" is in *Transposition and Other Addresses* (Bles, UK, 1949) and as *The Weight of Glory and Other Addresses* (Macmillan, US; paperback, Eerdmans, US). Also a handmade edition of "The Weight of Glory: with an introduction by Dr. Erik Routley" (Unicorn Press, Greensboro, North Carolina, 1977).
4. Bles, UK, 1943; Eerdmans, US.
5. One of Lewis's pupils claims this was Major Lewis's habit, when he was his brother's secretary.
6. *The Ring of Truth* (Hodder and Stoughton, UK, 1969), p. 117.

Chapter Twelve
Memories
H.C. Chang

1. Edinburgh University Press, 1955.
2. Edinburgh University Press, 1973.
3. Edinburgh University Press, 1977.
4. *Aureng-zebe:* a tragedy by Dryden.
5. About Sir Guyon losing his horse.
6. The Bodley Head, UK, 1955; Macmillan, US, 1955; paperback, Collier, US.

Chapter Thirteen
Surprise Encounter
Naoyuki Yagyu

1. *Miracles* (Collins, 1980), p. 58.

Chapter Fourteen
Poet to Poet
Ruth Pitter

1. This medal is usually conferred by the Poet Laureate at a public meeting. But this time, 1956, because Miss Pitter was the first woman to win it, the Queen conferred it and received her singly at Buckingham Palace as she receives others on these occasions. Emerging from the drawing room afterwards, Miss Pitter encountered Dr. Albert Schweitzer, the Alsatian medical missionary. He was the next to go in. He had won the Order of Merit. "I am glad," says Miss Pitter, "I had the presence of mind to curtsy to him as I had to the Queen; and he bowed."

2. *Poems* (Crescent Press, UK; Macmillan, US, 1968); *End of Drought* (Barrie and Jenkins, UK, 1975).

3. Bodleian Library, Oxford.

4. Uttered by Mr. Dyson to Miss Pitter and used with her permission.

5. Oxford University Press, UK and US, 1958.

6. Now incorporated in *Mere Christianity* (Fontana, UK, 1975; Macmillan paperback, US).

7. These Narnian tales are now selling more than a million copies a year.

Chapter Fifteen
The Fun of the Thing
A.J.P. Taylor

1. *Letters,* July 1-16, 1924 and August 30, 1929.

2. Winston Churchill agrees with Lewis. About Lord Macaulay, Churchill writes, "This historian with his captivating style and devastating self-confidence was the prince of literary rogues. He always preferred the tale to the truth, and smirched the glorified great men and garbled documents according as they affected his drama" *My Early Life,* p. 119.

3. *The Letters of C.S. Lewis to Arthur Greeves*, edited by Walter Hooper (Collins, 1979; Macmillan, NY, 1979), pp. 379, 381.

4. Ibid., p. 477.

5. On this point, Professor Clyde S. Kilby, author-editor of five books about Lewis, tells me, "I *do* think Lewis believed that."

6. *Letters to Arthur Greeves,* Hooper.

7. *God in the Dock* (Eerdmans, 1970), p. 55.

Chapter Seventeen
The Mystery
Malcolm Muggeridge

1. *C.S. Lewis: A Biography* (Collins, UK; Harcourt, Brace, Jovanovich, US, 1974).
2. *The Observer,* July 7, 1974.
3. Austin Kark, a pupil of Lewis's, speaking on "I Call it Joy: C.S. Lewis Remembered," BBC, January 29, 1978.
4. See chapter by Norman Bradshaw, pp. 17-27.
5. *A Preface to Paradise Lost* (Oxford University Press, UK and US, paperback, 1971), Chapter XVIII, last page.
6. *Letters of C.S. Lewis* (Bles, London, 1966; Harcourt, Brace and World, New York, 1966) letter dated March 13, 1921, p. 55.
7. "After dinner, things improved considerably: Dyson took us to a little book lined study, where we had coffee and he read an imitation of Pope which he had written, and which I thought good, tho' here again I was handicapped by not understanding most of the allusions . . . I was just getting comfortable when he uttered the fatal 'Shall we join the ladies?' which put me out the more, as I had not been expecting it. (J afterwards said, 'I wonder what would have happened if one had just said Well, I think we're very comfortable where we are')" *Brothers & Friends: An Intimate Portrait of C.S. Lewis; the Diaries of Major Warren Hamilton Lewis,* edited by Clyde S. Kilby and Marjorie Lamp Mead (Harper and Row, 1982), p. 99.
8. Fontana, UK, 1975; Macmillan paperback, US.
9. Fontana, UK, 1970; Macmillan paperback, US.
10. Bles, UK; Macmillan paperback, US.

Chapter Eighteen
Impact
Stephen Schofield

1. *J.R.R. Tolkien: A Biography* by Humphrey Carpenter (Allen & Unwin, UK, 1977; Houghton Mifflin, US, 1977). See chapter entitled, "Jack," which relates Tolkien's fluctuating friendship with Lewis.
2. *The New Republic,* April 29, 1944.

3. Quoted by Vernon Sproxton on BBC program, "I Call it Joy: C.S. Lewis Remembered," January 29, 1978.

4. December, 1947.

5. The alleged erroneous writing is in *Surprised by Joy* (Bles, UK, 1955; Harcourt, Brace, Jovanovich, US, paperback). See the schoolboy chapters. The correction is in Major Lewis's memoir in *Letters of C.S. Lewis* (Bles, UK, 1966; Harcourt, Brace, Jovanovich, UK, 1966), p. 5.

6. Bles, UK, 1947; Macmillan, US, 1947; with a revision of chapter three, Fontana, UK, 1960; Macmillan paperback.

7. Professor Naoyuki Yagyu, chancellor of Kanto Gakuin University, Yokohama, to the editor, August 30, 1982.

8. *Born Again* (Fleming H. Revell, Old Tappan, NJ) and *Life Sentence* (Fleming H. Revell, Old Tappan, NJ); both by Charles Colson.

9. John Lane, UK, 1943; Macmillan, US, 1944; as *Voyage to Venus,* Pan Books, UK, 1953; Macmillan paperback, US.

10. Macmillan, US, 1949.

11. Harcourt, Brace, Jovanovich, 1979.

12. Published in the US as *The Case for Christianity* and now incorporated in *Mere Christianity.*

13. These include *The Christian World of C.S. Lewis* (Marcham Manor, 1965), *Letters to an American Lady* (Eerdmans, 1967; Eerdmans, paper; Hodder and Stoughton, UK, 1969); *A Mind Awake: An Anthology of C.S. Lewis* (Bles, London, 1968); *C.S. Lewis—Images of His World* (Eerdmans, 1973; Hodder and Stoughton, London, 1974); *Images of Salvation in the Fiction of C.S. Lewis* (Shaw, 1978) and, with Marjorie Lamp Mead, *Brother & Friend: An Intimate Portrait of C.S. Lewis; the Diaries of Major Warren Hamilton Lewis.*

14. See *C.S. Lewis: A Biography* by Roger Lancelyn Green and Walter Hooper (Collins, UK, 1973; Harcourt, Brace, Jovanovich, US, 1973), p. 223. *A Preface to Paradise Lost* (Oxford University Press, UK and US, 1975).

15. Oxford University Press, US, to editor Stephen Schofield.

16. Chapter Thirteen.

17. *Letters of C.S. Lewis* (Bles, UK, 1966; Harcourt, Brace, Jovanovich, US, 1966).

18. See article by Jill Freud in Chapter Six, pp. 55-59.

19. *They Stand Together* edited by Walter Hooper (Collins, UK,

Macmillan, US, 1979).

20. *Letters to an American Lady* (Eerdmans, US, 1967; paperback, Eerdmans). (UK, Hodder and Stoughton, 1969.)

21. June 25, 1963.

22. To editor Stephen Schofield, July 21, 1967.

23. Harper and Row, US, 1976; Sheldon Press, UK, 1977.

24. *A Severe Mercy* (Hodder and Stoughton, UK; Harper and Row, US, 1977; Bantam paperback, US; Hodder paperback, US, 1979).

25. In addition to the number of universities, a fair criterion is *The Times* and *Le Monde,* both top-quality newspapers. The long-established *Times* has been losing money heavily for years. *Le Monde,* born only in 1945, has far surpassed *The Times* in circulation and actually limits its advertising in order to avoid becoming too dependent on it.

26. *Le probléme de la souffrance* (Desclée de Brouwer, Paris, 1950), used with permission.

27. Brother Stanislas of Monks Corner, South Carolina, in a letter in the New York C.S. Lewis *Bulletin,* June 1976, p. 18.

28. *The Life and Works of David Lindsay,* by Bernard Sellin (Cambridge University Press, New York, 1981).

29. *Letters of C.S. Lewis* (Harcourt, Brace, Jovanovich, 1966), p. 205.

30. Letter to Ruth Pitter, January 4, 1941.

31. Espasa-Calpo, Madrid, 1977.

32. See *Quarterly Notes on Christianity and Chinese Religion and Culture,* XX, No. 1, 1977.

33. The *Bulletin* of the New York C.S. Lewis Society, May, 1976, p. 8.

34. *The New York Times,* page one, general news section, December 10, 1976.

35. *The Achievement of C.S. Lewis* by Thomas Howard (Shaw, 1980).

36. "Fifty million copies": Walter Hooper, quoted in an article by James Munson in *The Canadian Churchman,* May, 1981.

37. Leonard Blake: to the editor, September 15, 1982.

Chapter Nineteen
Oxford Loses a Genius
Stephen Schofield

1. "When Lewis's *Allegory of Love* was published in 1936 it was

instantly recognized as a work of genius"—Sir David Hunt to editor Stephen Schofield, January 21, 1981.

2. *The Right to Know: The Rise of the World Press* by Francis Williams, "The BBC Misses an Opportunity," p. 125 (Longmans, London, 1969; not published in the US).

3. *English Literature in the Sixteenth Century* (Oxford University Press), p. 62.

4. *The New Anatomy of Britain* by Anthony Sampson (Hodder and Stoughton, 1971).

5. *Dangerous Estate: The Anatomy of Newspapers* by Francis Williams, chapter fifteen (Longmans Green, London, 1957; Macmillan, New York).

6. See *C.S. Lewis: A Biography* by Roger Lancelyn Green and Walter Hooper (Collins, UK; Harcourt, Brace, Jovanovich, US, 1974), p. 280. They use a stronger word: antipathy. Again, speaking in London, Mr. Green said, "Lewis was one of the most hated men in Oxford."

7. [Dean] Stuart Barton Babbage in *C.S. Lewis: Speaker and Teacher,* edited by Carolyn Keefe (Zondervan, US, 1971; Hodder and Stoughton, UK, 1974), p. 75.

8. *C.S. Lewis: A Biography* by Roger Lancelyn Green and Walter Hooper (Collins, UK; Harcourt, Brace, Jovanovich, US, 1974), p. 280.

9. *Letters of C.S. Lewis* edited by W.H. Lewis (Bles, UK; Harcourt, Brace, Jovanovich, US, 1966), November 22, 1931.

10. Lewis knew he deserved a professorship. Even at the age of thirty-six, when a vacancy occurred at the University of Birmingham, he knew he would be a strong candidate. He did not apply only because he did not want to live in Birmingham. *Brothers & Friends: An Intimate Portrait of C.S. Lewis; The Diaries of Major Warren Hamilton Lewis* edited by Clyde S. Kilby and Marjorie Lamp Mead (Harper & Row, 1982), p. 163.

11. Because this was a major turning point of Lewis's career, I asked two Lewis pupils about Dr. Starkie. One pupil responded: "Enid Starkie, a don, was an Oxford character, weird as they come. I believe she had it in for Lewis on a majestic scale. She was one of the prime figures, if not the prime figure, in organizing the movement that denied Lewis the professorship of poetry in Oxford." The other replied: "Enid Starkie, of Dublin, Ireland, became a fellow of Somerville College, Oxford, and reader of French literature from the 1940s to the 1960s. She moved in a

more 'way-out' and hedonist set than Lewis. She dressed very flamboyantly and colorfully. She wrote a book about Rimbaud, her favourite poet. There is a story of someone saying, 'There goes Enid— dressed in all the colors of the Rimbaud!' "

12. For full details, see *Enid Starkie* by Joanna Richardson (John Murray, UK; Macmillan, US, 1973), p. 88.

13. Bailey, with a major in Greek from Columbia University, became Russian and German liaison officer to Eisenhower's deputy, General Walter Bedell Smith, at SHAEF; served as interpreter and translator at the surrender in Berlin; subsequently a pupil of Lewis's and graduated with a BA and MA from Oxford University in 1949.

14. *C.S. Lewis: Speaker and Teacher* edited by Carolyn Keefe (Zondervan, US, 1971; Hodder and Stoughton, UK, 1974), p. 79.

15. *C.S. Lewis: A Biography* by Roger Lancelyn Green and Walter Hooper (Collins, UK; Harcourt, Brace, Jovanovich, US, 1974), p. 280.

16. I declare the truth without display of fine words or wisdom. First Corinthians 2:1, *The New English Bible* (Oxford University Press; Cambridge University Press, 1961).

17. To editor Stephen Schofield, July 21, 1967. *Hinc illae lacrimae:* hence those tears.

18. *Letters to Malcolm, Chiefly on Prayer* (Bles, UK, 1964; Harcourt, Brace, Jovanovich, US), p. 63.

19. To editor Stephen Schofield, October 8, 1981.

20. *C.S. Lewis: Speaker and Teacher* edited by Carolyn Keefe (Zondervan, US, 1971; Hodder and Stoughton, UK, 1974), p. 91.

21. These talks, first published in Britain as *Broadcast Talks* and in the US as *The Case for Christianity,* are now rewritten for the first part of *Mere Christianity.* I think the originals are more clearly written. It was an original that I bought as a present for my father. I wrote to Lewis and told him this. He replied that he hoped the rewritten version was better. Even now, I think not. Of those original talks, I would not change a comma.

22. *C.S. Lewis: Speaker and Teacher,* p. 99.

23. Associate Professor Lionel Adey in the New York C.S. Lewis Society *Bulletin,* Vol. 8, No. 5, March, 1977, p. 2. As his source, he gives Holin Hardie, Fellow of Magdalen College.

24. "Aristocratic Crumble," *The Dalhousie Review* (Halifax, Nova Scotia), Vol. 51, No. 1.

25. *They Stand Together: The Letters of C.S. Lewis to Arthur Greeves* (Collins, 1979), edited by Walter Hooper, editor's note, p. 40 (Macmillan, US).

26. *Letters of C.S. Lewis* edited by W.H. Lewis (Bles, UK, 1966; Harcourt, Brace, Jovanovich, US, 1966), May 10, 1921.

27. Milton Waldman, to editor Stephen Schofield, January 5, 1976. Mr. Waldman did not say who made this remark. At Lewis's invitation, Mr. Waldman, a writer, lived for some time at Magdalen College in the rooms once occupied by Oscar Wilde.

The Martyrs' Memorial, one of the most beautiful monuments in Oxford, is to Cranmer, Ridley, and Latimer, all prominent churchmen who were burned to death near the monument.

28. To editor Stephen Schofield, in Oxford, July 21, 1967.

29. To editor Stephen Schofield, in his residence in Westminster Abbey cloisters, London, August 6, 1967.

30. Letter to Sheldon Vanauken, February 20, 1955. See *A Severe Mercy* by Sheldon Vanauken (Hodder and Stoughton, UK; Harper & Row, US), p. 187.

31. *They Stand Together: Letters to Arthur Greeves* (Macmillan, US; Collins, 1979), March 26, 1958.

32. Both these laws were abolished in 1948.

33. *20th Century*, 1948.

34. This statement is attributed to Helen Gardner by Associate Professor Lionel Adey in "C.S. Lewis: The Man and What He Stood For" in the New York C.S. Lewis Society *Bulletin*, Vol. 8, No. 5, March, 1977, p. 2. Professor Adey tells me, "Miss Gardner was for many years a Professor of English at Oxford and an old colleague of Lewis's," and that "the word 'demeaned' was my attempt to reflect not her view but that of Lewis's many and bitter opponents in Oxford"—to editor Stephen Schofield, August 22, 1977.

Chapter Twenty
The Master: George MacDonald
Stephen Schofield

1. *Phantastes* (Bannatyne Books, 1975).

2. From the introduction by C.S. Lewis to *George MacDonald: An Anthology* (Bles, 1955), used with permission.

3. This chapter has been confirmed by a MacDonald scholar, the Reverend John Pridmore, chaplain of King Edward's School, Witley, Surrey. Mr. Pridmore spent one holiday at Yale University reading the MacDonald letters; another holiday at the University of Edinburgh, reading MacDonald manuscripts; and has collected most MacDonald books from second-hand shops.

4. *George MacDonald and His Wife* by Greville MacDonald (Allen & Unwin, London, 1924), chapters three to six, used with permission of Curwin, Jessopp and James, Solicitors, London.

5. "American violation of the International Copyright Law was a scandal"—Henry Fairlie in *The American Scholar,* winter issue, 1976-1977. A current instance is that of Ace Books which in 1965 published J.R.R. Tolkien's *Lord of the Rings* without permission of author or publisher. See Tolkien's biography by Humphrey Carpenter (Allen & Unwin, UK; Houghton Mifflin, US; Methuen, Toronto, 1977), VI, 3.

6. *Preaching in Theory and Practice* by the Reverend Samuel McComb; in a footnote on page 49 of *Reminiscences of a Specialist* by Greville MacDonald (Allen & Unwin, London, 1932), quoted with permission.

7. *Public Speaking* by Dale Carnegie (The World's Work, 1964), p. 120.

8. *A Rough Shaking* (Blackie & Sons, Glasgow, 1897), p. 23, used with permission.

9. *Reminiscences of a Specialist,* p. 321, used with permission.

10. The sacred present: I called up the Reverend John Pridmore about this. He said, "Yes, lots of people turned to MacDonald in anxiety about their future, and MacDonald always told them the path to peace lay in doing the next thing to be done. He once said that work done is of more consequence to the future than the foresight of an archangel"—to editor Stephen Schofield, May, 1980.

11. *Self-Denial, Second Series, Unspoken Sermons.* A selection of Unspoken Sermons has been published under the title of *Creation in Christ,* edited by Rolland Hein (Harold Shaw Publishers, 1976).

12. Margaret Sayer, reviewing *The Harmony Within: The Spiritual Vision of George MacDonald* by Rolland Hein (Eerdmans, Grand Rapids, Michigan, 1982) in *The Canadian C.S. Lewis Journal,* Winter, 1983.

Chapter Twenty-One
Letters to an Editor
Stephen Schofield

1. "Though one way or another C.S. Lewis wrote quite a lot about himself, and has been much written about, he has remained a somewhat inscrutable figure, at least to me. Nor can it be said that Roger Lancelyn Green and Walter Hooper, in their otherwise excellent biography, succeed in wholly dispelling this inscrutability. They are perhaps too conscientious, too careful, too respectful, to get under Lewis's guard and penetrate his defences"—Malcolm Muggeridge in *The Observer*. (See chapter three, "Impressions of a Pupil," and chapter seventeen, "The Mystery.")

2. T.D. Weldon.

3. K.B. McFarlane (1903-1966).

4. *They Stand Together: The Letters of C.S. Lewis to Arthur Greeves (1914-1963)* edited by Walter Hooper (Collins, UK; Macmillan, US, 1979), p. 231.

5. Ibid., p. 449.

6. *C.S. Lewis: Speaker and Teacher* edited by Carolyn Keefe (Zondervan, US, 1971), p. 50.

7. The Lewis brothers talked about Al Capone. *Brothers & Friends: An Intimate Portrait of C.S. Lewis; The Diaries of Major Warren Hamilton Lewis* edited by Clyde S. Kilby and Marjorie Lamp Mead (Harper & Row, San Francisco, 1982), p. 108.

8. *The White Cliffs* by Alice Duer Miller (Methuen, London, fifth impression 1941), p. 49.

9. Charles Lindbergh and family sailed for England in December, 1935.

10. *Of Time and the River* by Thomas Wolfe (Scribners, New York, 1935), p. 660.

11. *George MacDonald and His Wife* by Greville MacDonald (Allen & Unwin, London, 1924). See chapters three to six.

12. Henry Fairlie in *The American Scholar*, winter issue, 1976-1977.

13. Lewis mentions in the preface to his *George MacDonald: An Anthology* (Bles, London, 1946), p. 10, that he has read Greville MacDonald's *George MacDonald and His Wife*.

14. *George MacDonald: An Anthology*, p. 10.

15. "Membership" (pp. 39-40) which is in *Transposition and Other*

Addresses (Bles, UK, 1949) and in *The Weight of Glory and Other Addresses* (Macmillan, US, 1949: paperback Eerdmans).

16. "Equality," *The Spectator,* August 27, 1943.

17. (Oxford University Press, 1954; paperback Penguin), pp. 15-16.

18. *Essais* III, vi.

19. Humphrey Gilbert's *Discourse,* cap. 10.

20. See chapter three, "Impressions of a Pupil," by Norman Bradshaw.

21. The newest and most complete biography of Joy Davidman is *Surprised Atheist* by Lyle M. Dorsett (Macmillan, New York, 1983). It is based extensively on the papers of both her and her first husband, William Lindsay Gresham, which are now a part of The Marion E. Wade Collection, Wheaton College, Wheaton, IL.

22. To editor Stephen Schofield, August 15, 1975.

23. Professor George Sayer to editor Stephen Schofield, November 10, 1982.

24. See chapter two, "The Butcher."

25. Once, when Joy was telling Lewis that in the event of her death she wanted her sons to be amply endowed, she emphasized the point with a hard wallop of her walking stick across the top of the kitchen table.

26. *Letters of C.S. Lewis* (Bles, London; Harcourt, Brace & World, New York, 1966) and *Letters to an American Lady* edited by Clyde Kilby (Eerdmans paperback 1968).

27. Under the pseudonym N.W. Clerk: Faber and Faber, London, 1961; Seabury, New York, 1963; as by C.S. Lewis, same publishers, 1964.

28. See *"The New York Times* versus C.S. Lewis" in *The National Review,* October 12, 1979.